45 And Still Alive!
The Unique and Witty Car Experiences of Two Friends

Preface

This is a book dedicated to all car owners who have their own personal experiences with their cars (both good and bad).

Through this book we hope to share our combined experiences, while in the process, create a smile or two.

Note that the number "45" from the title is not intended to imply someone's age. Rather, it represents the number of cars that we have owned throughout the years.

Enjoy and happy driving!

1968 Buick Opel Kadett – "Hot Fun in the Summertime"

It was a cold day in January 1975. My fellow classmates could not understand why I was taking my driver's test in January. The fact of the matter is, I was younger than everyone else since I was born at the end of December and my mom had chosen to send me to school in kindergarten as a four-year-old.

But nonetheless it was time for me to take my drivers test – in January. What happens in January? Well of course, it snows! It snowed on the day of my driver's test so the motor vehicle office postponed my test. And again, it snowed; except this time, there was no cancellation. I just had to take the test in the snow. Boy did I get lucky with that. I took my drivers test and I was able to pass it. Now it was time to look for a car. Somehow my budget for a car ended up being only $400; what was I going to get for $400?

I searched the classified ads (there was no Internet at that time). I found all sorts of cars for $400 - cars that didn't run, cars that didn't have engines, cars that needed a paint job, cars that didn't have paint, cars that had no engine or paint. What was I to do?

Alas, I found what I was looking for! A red 1968 Buick Opel Kadett with a black interior. It had power nothing. I mean nothing! No power steering, no power brakes, no power windows, no power seats, no air conditioning. It didn't even have a radio. The manufacturer referred to this as a "radio delete." I suppose delete meant that it was a feature. Believe me, there was absolutely no feature about this car.

So I found a car to buy, went to the owner's house, turned in my $400, picked up my car and title. I then proceeded to drive around my hometown in my new car. By "new" I meant new to me. Believe me, it was the furthest thing from a new car.

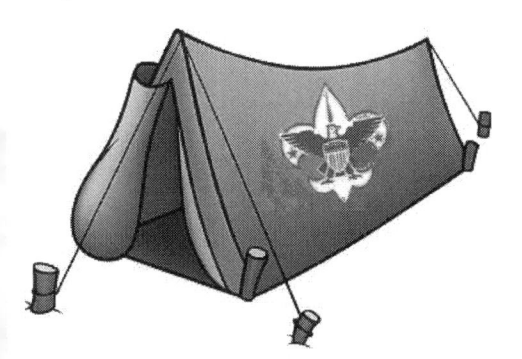

Fast forward to the summer of 1975. Since I was a Boy Scout, it was time to go to summer camp. How awesome - I get to drive my new car to summer camp! However, what I didn't know was that the car was about to become a real nudge.

I pulled into the camp parking lot to show off my car to my fellow scouts and camp leaders. One of my friends wanted to go for a ride with me. "No problem," I said. "Just hop in and I'll give you a ride down the road."

While driving down the road I noticed the car started to run very erratically. Then the car began to shutter. Finally the car stalled. I figured, okay, I should just be able to restart it. Well that didn't happen. It turns out the car needed a carburetor AND a starter motor.

I couldn't afford AAA insurance at the time and cell phones hadn't been invented yet, so my friend and I decided to push the car back to the camp. Except there was one problem: On the way back there was a hill that we had to get up with only two of us to push. Then I put my junior-mechanic thinking cap on and used my experience from my local Getty gas station. Since the car had a four speed manual transmission it's a known trick that a car with a manual transmission that will not start can be started by letting it roll down a hill, putting it into gear, and popping the clutch. So we proceeded to push the car up the hill, jump in the car, put it in gear and pop the clutch. One more problem developed. Since I've never done this before I wasn't able to pop the clutch quick enough to ignite the cylinders and start the engine. Getting the car back to camp felt like it would become a major accomplishment but the fun had only just begun.

As a mentioned earlier, I had worked at a Getty gas station as a junior mechanic. I had done things like tune-ups, tire changes, tire rotations, oil changes, exhaust work and some brake work among other things. But I had never changed the starter motor or carburetor in a car. It was about to...

One of my friends drove me into town to look for an auto parts dealer. Finding a starter motor and carburetor for this car wasn't too hard as the car was only seven years old. And the adults at the camp owned a myriad of tools that they could lend to me. I do not recall there being any car ramps at the time so we had to jack the car up and put the car on jack stands to replace the starter.

After I completed installing these two parts, I was ready to roll. Imagine, I was ready to take a date in my first car! We went to see a movie and ate at a diner. So we drove to the nearest theater which was about 25 miles away. Needless to say the camp was in a very remote area of the state. So what movie did I take my date to see? JAWS. Probably not the best movie to take a girl to in the summertime.

After seeing the movie, we got back into the car and I was ready to drive to the diner. I then paused for a moment and out of complete shock I could not believe my eyes. I noticed coolant dripping from the bottom of my engine compartment. Do not tell me that I need a new radiator hose. Nope! It was my water pump. Now this car was beginning to get on my nerves.

Over the next few days I proceeded to take the same steps that I did with the starter motor and carburetor except that I had to buy and replace a water pump. Of course, they only sold new (not rebuilt) water pumps, so by now I had spent more money on replacement parts than the car cost me to buy.

Well, I believed at that point that I was beyond the car being a nuisance. I was beginning to think it was a real lemon. I wondered why they called bad cars lemons, perhaps because of the sourness of the lemon or the annoying yellow color. Or maybe because the lemon will burn you if touched, not unlike the way I was burned by my Opel. Not sure which one but it became clear to me this car was a lemon.

One would think that starter motor, carburetor, and water pump failures were bad enough. What I proceeded to experience over the next month I would not want to wish on my worst enemy.

The next thing to go took place on a one lane highway with a speed limit of 55 miles an hour. I was actually probably going about 65 miles an hour, put on my left directional signal, and proceeded to make a left turn before the next oncoming car reached the intersection.

Upon making my turn, I needed to brake somewhat so that I could slow down to a safe speed. Except there was one problem – I had no brakes! Well I panicked. Realizing I was not slowing down enough in spite of downshifting, I pulled up on my emergency brake as hard as I could. I think if the emergency brake was not made out of steel I would've snapped it in two. I pulled up on it so hard, my car went into a spin. In fact, it went into approximately three spins – I think I did three 360s. From being good at math, that's over 1,000 degrees!

Now I was convinced that I owned a lemon. But what was still to come would top them all. You see, in a car that has rear wheel drive there is something that connects the transmission to the rear axle. It is called a driveshaft. And what allows a driveshaft to maneuver is called a U-joint. Why is it called a U-joint? Because when it fails, U are screwed.

For anyone who has experienced a U-joint failure, they would know that the car can only be driven backwards. Now imagine this: you have 25 miles to drive to get to the nearest mechanic, on a country road, BACKWARDS. That was the most terrifying incident I have ever experienced in my driving career. You think not seeing where you're going during dusk is the dangerous part? No. It's trying to steer in reverse.

At the time that I owned the Opel, I was living with my mom. One Saturday morning we needed to buy groceries but I also knew that I had a recent problem of starting my car. So I took out my voltmeter and confirmed that the battery needed to be replaced. Since I was working at Sears Auto Parts selling auto parts at the time, I simply walked into the back room, selected the right battery size, and proceeded to pay for it using my employee discount. I then brought the battery home, installed it in the car, and proceeded to go to the local Shop-Rite with my mom. The experience that followed only similarly happened to me once before in my lifetime, which happened to be prior to having received my driver's license.

I took my mom to the local Shop-Rite that was about three miles from our house. After food shopping we loaded the car with the groceries, made a left out of the parking lot and after about a ½ mile of driving I noticed something unusual taking place. THERE WERE FLAMES FLOWING OUT OF THE COWL OPENING IN THE HOOD. Apparently when I connected the positive cable to the battery I didn't tighten it enough. The cable came loose and shorted the battery on a piece of the frame in the engine compartment. I yelled to my mom to get out of the car - FAST. I too exited the car and quickly removed the air cleaner as the flames were now blazing from the opening of the carburetor. I took a handful of dirt from the ground and tossed it into the carburetor opening, thereby destroying my car!

A few months later, I was driving my mom to visit my sister who lived about 30-minutes away. We were about two-thirds of the way there, driving down a nicely wooded area, when all of a sudden the entire car started to shake furiously. It was as if a freight train had just barely missed hitting the car. No, I was in the process of losing one of my wheels.

As we were beginning to lose the wheel, my mom started to scream, "What the hell is happening?" I told her that I think it was related to a recent tire rotation that I had done by a local mechanic. Next thing you know, the wheel flies off of the car and collides with the nearest tree. Don't you know, after getting out of the car, I look down and see all five lug nuts sitting on the side of the road? Apparently the mechanic didn't tighten the lug nuts on the one wheel – AT ALL.

In the end, it wasn't the starter motor, it wasn't the water pump, it wasn't the brakes or the U joint that did in the Opel. Nope, that dopey looking red car with the black interior, no air-conditioning and power NOTHING was done in by ME! And boy was I glad to final get rid of that piece of junk.

1974 Vega – "Back on the Road Again"

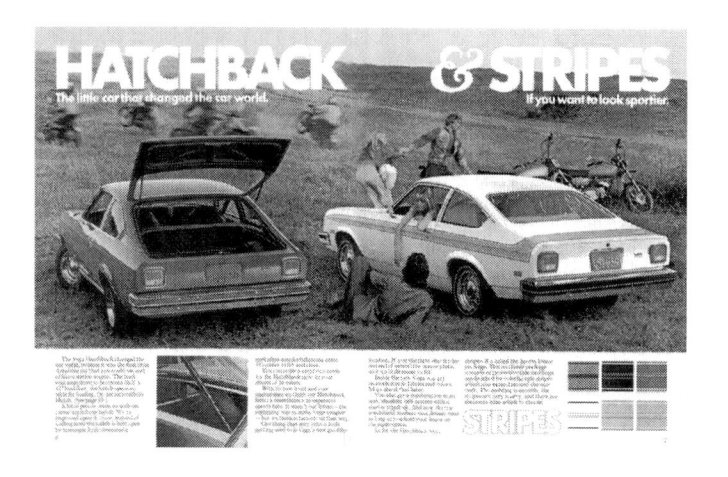

Up to this point, I owned what I thought were American cars. The "Buick" Opel and the "Pontiac" Firebird. Not so. While the Buick was branded as an American car, it was technically made in Germany. Nonetheless, it sounded American, so I decided to keep the American thing going. I bought myself a Chevy.

Now, understand that the Vega is not your ordinary Chevy. You see, in the early 70's Chevy had this bright idea that if they manufacture the engine block with a lightweight material, the car will get better gas mileage. Perhaps so, especially in light of the oil crisis that the economy was suffering through during those times. Herein lies the rub: ALUMINUM MELTS WITH HEAT.

Aluminum has a melting point of about 1200° Fahrenheit. Internal engine temperatures can run as high as 3600° Fahrenheit. HELLO? CHEVY ENGINEERS, WHAT WERE YOU THINKING?

That car didn't last long. I sold it to a friend who ultimately experienced its demise shortly after he bought it. In the process I could have lost a friend, but as it turned out, I lost another American car. It was now time for a change. Back on the road again…

1970 Pontiac Firebird Esprit – "Out of the Frying Pan and into the Firebird"

So I finally got rid of my Opel. After that boondoggle, I figured that ANY other car would be better than what I had before. I was almost correct.

Unlike a four-door sedan with power nothing, I was in the mood for a sportier car. I was working at a department store in Paramus New Jersey that hasn't been in business since the 1980s. One of my coworkers just happened be selling his car, a 1970 Pontiac Firebird. I asked him what he was asking for the car and he told me $1200. I looked at the car, he let me take it for a ride, I looked at the engine compartment, and everything looked good to me as far as I could tell.

The owner told me that the price was not negotiable since the new owner (me) would be getting a nice car. I have to admit, the car was very sporty looking. The body was painted with a metallic silver color and the roof had a vinyl top on it. The interior was black and the transmission was a Powerglide, which is a two-speed transmission that back in the day (in the 1950s) was used in race cars. The car had a 350 cubic-inch engine with a two-barrel carburetor. The base model was the 2-door coupe and came standard with a 250 CID six-cylinder engine that produced 155 horsepower. When a buyer upgraded to the next Firebird option, which was the Esprit (the model that I had purchased from my co-worker), a 350 CID V8 was included standard that produced 255 horsepower.

So now I finally had a sports car that I wanted. It wasn't a Trans Am; it wasn't a Pontiac 400; but, it was an Esprit and it was MINE. I decided to add a few amenities to my new car: air shocks in the back, rally wheels (which I believe was standard but was not included in the car), and fog lights. Of those upgrades, the only one that I regret buying was the air shocks since they give the car a very hard ride. Nonetheless, the car looked really "neat."

Mechanically speaking compared to the Opel the car didn't give me much trouble. The only thing that I needed to replace was the starter motor; but that's when my luck ran out. As it turns out the previous owner was a bit of a racer with that car. I bought the car on July 1, 1976; by February of 1977, I was beginning to experience what I thought may have been transmission problems. I brought my car to AAMCO, the leading authority in transmission repairs. I'll never forget the advertising jingle:

" Double A…beep beep… MCO." It was because of that jingle that I brought my car to the company for transmission diagnosis. I guess I was a roadrunner fan. Anyway, after spending an hour looking at my transmission the technician came out to give me the bad news. It was going to cost me more than what I paid for the car to rebuild the transmission; that's right over $1500.

Okay, I figured out my investments so far were the cost of the car, the starter motor, and the transmission rebuilt: a total of about $3000. Then the real trouble began.

Unfortunately for me, I was living next to a neighbor who had severe emotional problems. She was actually kicked out of her last apartment complex because the neighbors created and signed a petition to have her removed, or else they were all going to move. No matter who she lived next to, she created major problems for them. In my case, I suppose she was jealous of my car. I went out to my car one day and I found a really gooey substance splattered all over my car. It turned out to be naval jelly, which is a substance that is normally used to remove rust from metal. In my case it removed paint from metal. I needed a complete paint job. I looked high and low for a place that would pay my car for a cheap price; I finally found one: Earl Sheib. Earl Sheib was a company that would paint cars for very little money. In my case, I recall spending only $500. However, that was $500 more that I spent on the car. My total was up to about $3500.

While working at a department store in Paramus, I ran into a customer that rebuilt engines. The reason why this interested me was that the Firebird had over 100,000 miles on it. I figured its compression was getting low. So I asked this customer what he would charge for a valve job. Now realize that I was not sending out the heads to have them reconditioned at a machine shop. This was someone was going to manually replace the valves himself, as he proceeded to do over a several month period in his garage. I remember visiting him on many occasions in his garage, wishing and praying to get my car back. Of course, I wasn't going to say anything to him. Wouldn't want 'em to "mistakenly" install the rocker arms in the heads in the wrong direction.

I got a quote from him in the amount of $500. When all was said and done, the job ended up costing $750. I suppose that this money was a good investment if some of the compression was restored in the engine. Little did I know, I was in for more trouble.

You see unless you completely rebuild an engine, you always run the risk of worsening one problem after you have fixed another. In this case that's exactly what happened. Yes I did restore compression in the heads, but so much so that I started to experience what is known as "blow by." Blow by is a condition where gas leaks past the pistons under pressure. In my case, this pressure was the increase in compression caused by the rebuilt heads. The piston's rings could no longer contain this pressure. The symptom that the car was exhibiting was extreme oil leakage in and around the PCV (Positive Crankcase Ventilation) valve.

Now I knew that I simply could not afford to have the rings replaced as this would have probably been the most expensive single repair that I would have invested in this car. So, sadly, I decided to sell my "sports car." The best I could manage was $500 since the engine was so old. By now, the car had about 120,000 miles on it. Time for my next car...

1978 Datsun B210, 1983 Toyota Tercel, 1982 Mercury LN7 – "Fun With Small Cars"

Okay, so I had to give up my dream car. What could be worse? Can you say "boredom?"

My next few cars were uneventful, although my wife didn't think so in one case. The next car after the Firebird was a 1978 Datsun B210. A very boring, white car with a black interior. Okay, so it had air condition and an AM/FM cassette player. But it was just plain boring.

I only owned that car for a few years until we got married, at which time we bought a 1983 Toyota Tercel. At that time, I was working in New York City and commuted via the train so technically we only needed one car.

Now, the Tercel was supposed to be my wife's car. Note the word "supposed." The Tercel was a 3-door (third-door being a hatchback) with a 5-speed manual transmission.

There were three things that went wrong with the Tercel:
The carburetor kept breaking down to the point of no return. In spite of three rebuilds, it never did run right ever again
The clutch began to go. We couldn't afford to replace the clutch, so we kept forging on.

Last but certainly not least, my wife's sanity almost went at the expense of the Tercel. You see, my wife never drove a car with a manual transmission. So I figured, Okay, I can save the money we would spend on a driving instructor and going ahead and teach her myself. WRONG ANSWER.

One day after having given her about a dozen or so "lessons," I received a frantic phone call at work. I was thinking that it had to be something bad. Well, my wife was okay (physically), but if I was standing next to her instead of being on the phone, I would be writing this chapter right now.

She told me the car "bucked" all the way to and from work on her first day of taking it to her job. That was also the last day that she did that...

Then I took ownership of the Tercel and I proceeded to shop for another American car (thinking of course it had to be related to the Tercel being a foreign made car).

So I drove to a local Ford dealership, looked at what they had in their used car lot and picked out a nice, sporty looking 1982 Mercury LN7. Now the LN7 is a cousin to the Ford EXP. You know, sport looking but nothing sporty about it? It had all of 80 horsepower. Count 'em, 80. Five of those and I got myself one fast car.

But since that was my wife's car, and it was automatic, we were both happy...for awhile until the troubles began.

You see, Ford designed their Mercury LN7 in a very interesting way. They positioned the fuel pump directly over the exhaust manifold. Besides being a fire danger, what proceeded to happen not once, not twice, but three different times was fuel pump failure due to the seal drying out from the heat of the manifold. That problem, in and of itself, was probably enough to get rid of the car. Instead, I went back to the dealer to complain about this problem. They resolved the issue by mounting an electric fuel pump on the driver's side firewall. Problem with that? Very noisy. I was beginning to get sick of this car.

My wife was willing to put up with the whining noise that the electric pump would constantly make upon acceleration. But what ensued was the icing on the cake.

At one point while I was driving car which was rare since my car was the Tercel, I noticed what could be a transmission problem. The car would slip in and out of gear. Sure enough, I bring the car to a local AAMCO (sound familiar?) and the technician confirms the transmission need to be rebuilt. No wonder why the dealer was selling the car.

I tried selling the car back to dealership, but they wouldn't give me a good deal, in spite of the transmission expense that I just put into it. So I reneged and proceeded to write the CEO of Mercury a nice, long "spirited" letter. It was so long and spirited, I actually received a check in the mail for $2,500! That covered the cost of three fuel pumps and the transmission. It was now time to look for another car...

1982 Datsun 210, 1986 Hyundai Excel, 1993 Toyota Camry – "My Sometimes Impulsive Behavior"

Just at the time that I thought we needed a second car, I got a job in New York City. My brother-in-law owned a property that was literally 300 feet from the train station where the train line that I needed to take into the city was located. Great! We only need one car. One big problem with my idea...my Tercel had a manual transmission. Wait! I can teach my wife how to drive a stick shift.

One day I was at my desk at work in the city when I received a frantic phone call from my wife. All sorts of really bad things started to go through my mind. Was she attached, was she in a car accident, did something happen to one of our sons. No, it was my "idea." She said that while driving to work, the car bucked or stalled no less than 20 times – ONE WAY.

That was it. We needed a second car wit an automatic transmission. So we bought a red car with a black interior from a private owner. It was a 1982 Datsun 210. Seems reasonable, right? One big problem – a car with a black interior, in the summertime with NO air conditioning which was my wife's car who was driving our one-year-old son around. This did not make the wife happy AT

ALL. It think the car was named a "210" for a reason. That is about how many hours we owned it for.

We continued our search for a second card. How about this for another great idea? At that time, the Hyundai Excel was hitting the dealerships for the first time.

One thing I should have learned from my past – never buy anything that is a first year production. My idea? I went to a local Hyundai dealership and bought not one, but two "his and her" Excels! I put down two $500 down payments on them. Boy did I lose sleep that night! I went back to the dealer and the salesman graciously refunded my money in full after I explained to him my sometimes compulsive behavior.

Our next car turned out to be a 1985 Nissan Sentra.

The Sentra was an OK car. No major repairs. One interesting thing, though happened at the exact same time.

These cars were made pre-fuel injection so they both had carburetor fueled engines. The interesting thing was that both cars' carburetors died at the exact same time. By this time, I had moved out of the New York City job and worked in central New Jersey where public transportation from Northern New Jersey (where we were still living) was not practical. Therefore, I depended on a car. By this time, we had our first son so my wife decided to be a stay-at-home mom. But I still needed a car.

I decided to keep both cars and had both carburetors rebuilt. Do you know that just about at the same time (again), BOTH carburetors died again! I couldn't take the chance of having either of the cars die on me again since I was beginning to take "personal" days at work and did not want to miss work at my job. So we traded both cars in at a local dealership and bought a two-year-old 1983 Toyota Camry. Wait till you hear this next story…

In 1985, I bought a two-year 1983 Toyota Camry station wagon from a local dealer I had a fairly good rapport with. I pride myself in (at least thinking) that I am a good negotiator with buying cars. So I paid $11,000 (which would be the equivalent of $25,000 at the time of this writing) for the car.

Actually, the Camry did us very well. Over the many years and the many trips that we took our family on, there were two weak spots on this car. For some reason, both the front and rear motor mounts kept breaking. I think between the front and rear mounts (which there were a total of 3 of as I recall), I replaced a total of about 8 mounts all together.

Then one interesting thing happened to me while ironically on the way to the repair shop to replace one of the motor mounts. The passenger side front coil spring snapped in half! The entire car was sagging so much that I almost couldn't negotiate the ride to the repair shop.

The only other trouble that I had with that car until its ultimate demise was that the distributor kept dying. It was replaced (with a non-OEM rebuild, unfortunately) a total of three times. But here's the story behind its demise:

My wife has a "craft cave" since our boys have moved out of the house and live out-of-state. So she wanted to outfit her room with furniture from a local IKEA retail store. She came with me with a list in hand, picked out every piece of shelving, desk, desk legs, night stand, light fixture, etc. and I proceeded to put as much of these item in our Camry has possible. Remember, this was a station wagon so it had a hatchback opening with fold-down rear seats. There was no "third row" seating in this are.

Her list was so large, I had to go home, drop her and "part 1" of the furniture off and drive back to IKEA to pick out and buy part 2.

The list was large, that even with the second trip the car was so full of IKEA objects, I thought the was going to explode from inside pressure.

Twenty-five dollars later (courtesy tip), an IKEA associate and I finally finished loading the car, and I was off. It is important to note that it was Memorial Day weekend and it was hot out! As I recall it was over 90% by the time I hit the road to go home.

I took the New Jersey turnpike to go home. Anyway that is familiar with that highway knows that the exits are far away from each other, unlike the Garden State Parkway where each one is a mile apart.

So I'm tooling along the highway when, all of sudden, the car starts to shudder. Now of course I'm thinking "Oh yeah, it's the distributor again." WRONG. The car never stalled, but I noticed it was taking more and more throttle to maintain the same speed. Finally, I was literally flooring the pedal so that I could maintain a speed of about 10 miles per hour. Needless to say, I began driving on the shoulder. About 15 minutes into my ordeal, I noticed a state trooper sitting on the side of the road, checking for speeders. Imagine this site: I slowly pull up in this completely loaded Camry, filled with IKEA s----, roll down my "fancy" power window and explained to the officer my dilemma. All that I requested of him was to allow me to continue tooling down the road so that I could get a tow from AAA once I made it off highway. Actually, I wanted to try and get it all the way home, but I was skeptical. His reply was that as long as I felt that I could do it safely, then go ahead.

The one big problem that I ran into was this: Imagine you're driving tops 10 miles per hour, and you approach an exit. Now folks behind you are not only pissed off at you for driving well below the minimum limit, but they are trying to exit in front of me as I creep along. DANGEROUS.

The next problem that I ran into was my engine began to overheat. In fact, with the pedal to the metal, I had that temperature gauge BURIED as far as I could go. Kinda reminds me of the Seinfeld episode where Kramer takes a new car for a ride with a dealer salesman and they begin to run out of gas. He decides to pass the exit to go back to dealership as he floors it, hand-in-hand with the salesman. The difference with me was there was no-one to "share" this wonderful experience with.

I made it off the turnpike and onto another local highway. Except this time, my luck ran out. No more shoulder to drive on. There was NO WAY I was going to drive 10 miles per hour on any highway! So I had to call AAA and had the car towed home.

Here is my theory on what went wrong with that car.

First, I think that either the timing belt slipped off of the pulley teeth OR the timing belt tensioner failed. By the time the temperature started to rise, I could have, in retrospect, pulled over and salvaged the car. My thinking? The distributor and motor mount failures. May she rest in peace...

1995 Ford Crown Victoria Police Interceptor – "No Crown Jewel"

My youngest son was of age to drive, so I decided to treat him to a nice car. I found a Crown Vic in the classifieds that look interesting since it was the police interceptor model.

I got a great deal on the car, not realizing what I was in store for. I only paid $1,300 (again, my "negotiation" skills kicked in). What I didn't realize what the litany of things that it needed. How's this for a list?:

The rear axle died
The transmission died
The car needed brakes, front and rear
The entire front-end was shot
The windshield was cracked (which of course I knew when I bought it – that is how I played my hand while negotiating)
The ignition switch went on it after a few months of ownership

Total repair costs? $13,000. Normally, this would be expensive for this list of repairs. But since this was a police interceptor model, the brakes and suspension were heavy duty and required heavy duty bucks to fix them.

Now when you add in the great deal that I paid for the car, it cost me a total of $14,300. The car ended up in an accident (thankfully everyone was ok). But the money pit finally ceased to exist!

1992 Toyota Corolla – "Living the Good Life"

At one point in my career I worked for AT&T, at the time the largest private (non-government) employer in the United States. In the early 1980's they employed about one million people. I worked at AT&T for a number of years in various New Jersey locations, one of them being in Bedminster, New Jersey. The year was 1996.

Imagine working in a location so large that there were two huge, mirror image buildings side by side, separated by an even larger parking lot. Day after day year after year, like clockwork, I parked in the exact same parking space. No exceptions. Then one day at around 5 PM I walked to my spot and to my shock, the car was gone. Gone! No trace of it. No motor oil leak, no cracked glass. Nothing!

I proceeded back into the building and quickly headed for the security department. I ended up speaking with a couple of security guards and I asked them if the property is protected with security cameras. One of them responded, "Sure does!" I proceeded to explain to them that my car was missing, so they checked their cameras and sure enough, found my car being stolen. "Yep, there goes your car; it was stolen at exactly 11:31:25 AM." "Thanks for that" I replied. And oh by the way, what is your job duties again (I didn't say that part to them, but I should have).

I later found out by local police that the thieves took a train from New York City, de-boarded at Convent Station near Morristown, stole a GMC Suburban, took their "laundry list" of cars to steal and proceeded and look for and find the largest parking lot in the area. At that time, the Bridgewater mall wasn't as large as our parking lot was. Five of the six thieves ended up stealing cars from our lot. Ironically, one of the cars was found down the road, [not so] sadly having run out of gas. That thief pulled into the nearest strip mall, abandoned the original stolen car, and proceeded to steal yet another car from the strip mall's lot.

Another irony…parked in between my lowly corolla at the time it was stolen were a late model Mercedes and an Acura. Guess the thieves had an affinity for Toyotas.

Long story short, my car was never recovered and according to the local FBI office, it was probably disassembled in Newark and shipped to one or more European location, "Living the Good Life."

1998 Nissan Altima – "One 'Minor' Issue"

Other than one "minor" issue, I must say that I have had quite a bit of good fortune with this car. That said, when the car had about 100,000 miles on it, the timing CHAIN broke. Timing belts break, timing chains usually do not. In the combined experience of myself, my friend (co-author of this book), and my mechanic friends at the local Meineke shop, none of us have ever experienced (or even knew of) a timing chain breakage.

I had three options after the chain broke: Junk the car, buy a used to be installed in this car, or having the engine remanufactured (essentially a new engine using the old parts). I went with door number three. She's been good to me even since.

1998 Corolla & 1999 Corolla – "The Best of the Best"

Can't say too much about these cars: They have 350,000 combined miles presently. The ONLY things that I have replaced on them? Each one had to have the hood latch cable replaced and the starter motors. That is it! Oh yeah, they are both the same color. That sure confused my neighbors!

1957 Chevy - "Edna"

After I had worked in Corporate America for a number of years and our children got older in age, I decided to treat myself to a couple of collector cars. One was a 1957 Chevy BelAir four door sedan, black with a white top and white posts (the roof support pillars). The engine-compartment was almost twice the size of the 283 cu inch engine that was in it. In fact, the gap between the radiator and the front frame was large enough to fit a man. I can attest to that from two perspectives, one inside and one outside. I have worked on the engine while squatting inside this compartment (as alluded to below). I have also witnessed this feat from afar. I was at a car show enjoying my lunch when, while walking on the way back from he food vendors there appeared a man squatting in this compartment of my car. When this brazen gentlemen why he was in there, he replied, "Oh, I just wanted to see what it would be like to work on the engine from in here." I proceeded to tell him to get the h--- out of my car!"

One day I was removing the stock 2-barrel carburetor so that I can send it out for a rebuild. There were four nuts that were attached to four bolts that were welded onto the engine block. In the process of removing the nuts and then the carburetor, one of the nuts fell into the intake manifold opening where the carburetor would normally be. Oh no! What is going to happen? What proceeded to happen was the wildest single incident that I ever experience with a car.

I started the engine, pulled out of my driveway, and drove to my mechanic. At one point I was waiting at a light waiting for it to turn green. Upon giving the car gas, a HUGE plume of blue smoke completely enveloped the car behind me. I sure felt sorry for the driver of the car behind me. I wouldn't be able to pick them out in a lineup, that's for sure.

My mechanic proceeded to pull every spark from the engine and found that the nut had apparently sheared off the top half of one of the spark plugs, which in turn went nuts (no pun intended) inside of the corresponding cylinder. This resulted in the plug remnant gauging a hole the size of between a quarter and a half dollar in the corresponding piston.

I explained what had happened to a neighbor friend who lived across the street from my house. I thought the car was done!. He said to me, "Well, you have three options: junk it, sell it as it is, or rebuild the engine." I replied, "Rebuild the engine? With me and which army?" He said that he and I would could do it together.

Bottom line, over a period of about 3 months, he and I spent a couple of hours each night working on that engine. We pulled the connecting rods from the bottom of the engine, from the oil pan side, reamed the top of the cylinders, honed the cylinder walls, replaced all of the pistons and compression/oil rings, etc. One interesting thing that I found out about my engine was that when I went to the machine shop to have the connecting rods to pistons, the gentleman at the shop said that this will not working. At first I thought we had done all of the work for nothing. He then told me that my engine had already been bored .040 over and that the standard size pistons that I ordered would not fit. I simply re-ordered the correct piston size and we were good to go. While I was at the shop, I also brought the heads which happened to be original to the car. They completely rebuilt he valve with modern seats and seals. What a difference these made! I was almost glad that this happened. I also had great conversations with my friend during the rebuilt. I am not sure that that wasn't the better of the two outcomes.

What a great experience for me since I had never rebuilt and engine this before! I am so careful when working near the carburetor now!

Three other great experiences I have had with this car: My car was in a wedding, a movie, and several parades with my sons. And by the way, the title of this chapter? I loved the car except that, well, my wife thinks she looked like an "Edna."

1969 Mustang
"The Bumble Bee"

My other collector car was a 1969 Mustang Grande. The Grande was the model that had simulated wood grain inside and the vinyl top. When I purchased the car, it was a wreck. Several panels were rusted through, the engine was tired, and the car was used as a daily driver.

With my engine rebuild experience with the '57 Chevy, I performed the following repairs/upgrades to the car:
Rebuilt heads
Rebuilt carburetor
Converted stock air cleaner to an open air cleaner with K&N filter
Electronic ignition kit (no more points or condenser)
Installed a Monte Carlo bar that helps prevent front-end wracking
Installed new shocks all around including heavy duty Monroe's complete with coil springs in the rear. This raised the car a bit and gave it a nice, sporty look.
High performance coil and ignition wires
Carburetor spacer for more air intake
Dual FlowMaster mufflers along with a cross-over pipe to allow exhaust transfer from both heads
New paint job with racing stripes (thanks to my son Dan for his "bumble bee" color choice
Sporty rims (the stock hubcaps looked terrible)
Repainted engine and engine compartment
Chromed out the engine: valve covers, air cleaner, oil dip stick, Monte Carlo bar, etc.

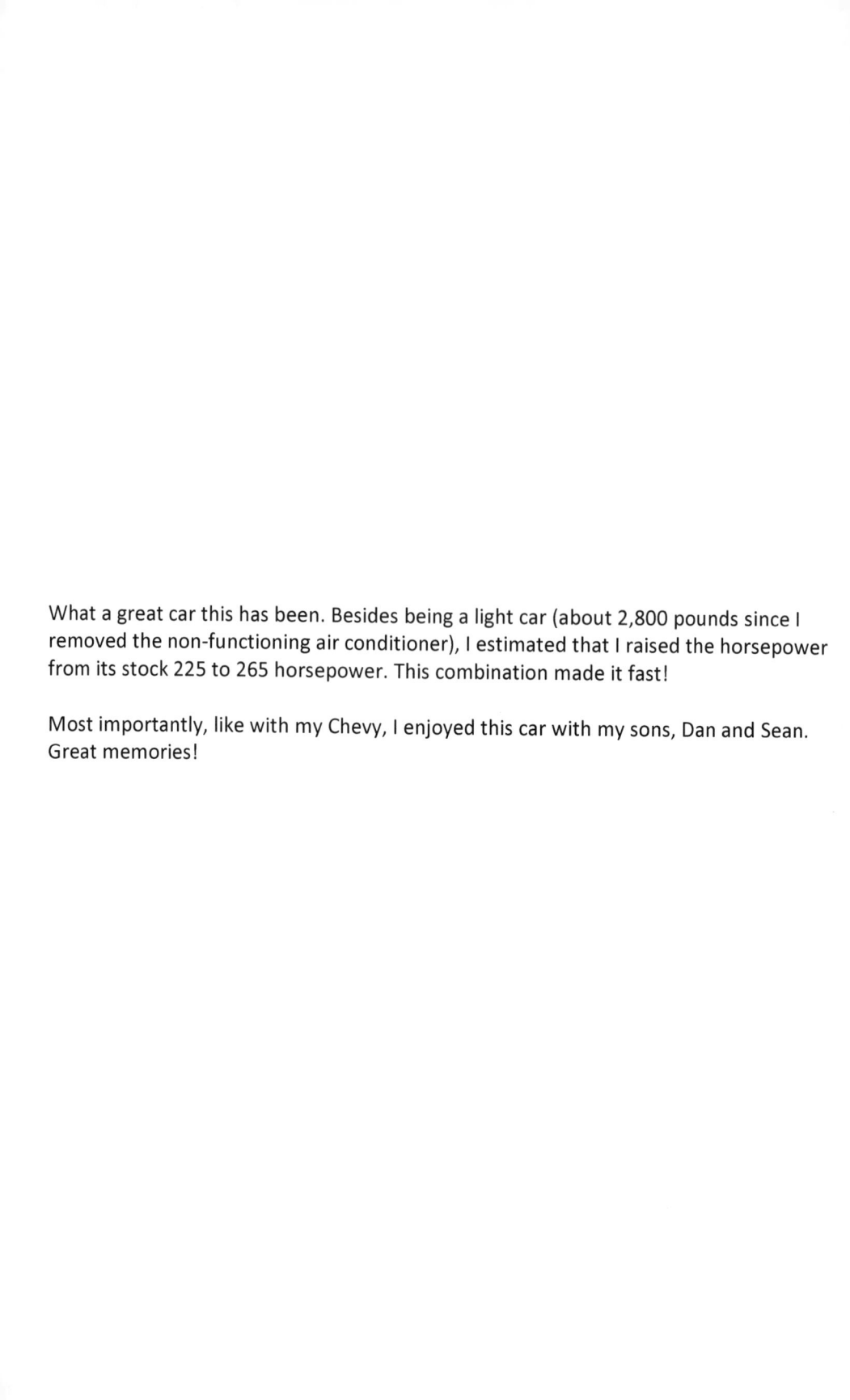

What a great car this has been. Besides being a light car (about 2,800 pounds since I removed the non-functioning air conditioner), I estimated that I raised the horsepower from its stock 225 to 265 horsepower. This combination made it fast!

Most importantly, like with my Chevy, I enjoyed this car with my sons, Dan and Sean. Great memories!

J-Cars of a Lifetime

Parents have a lot of influence over their children's choices in life. I have found this to be true in the automotive arena as well. Most of my vehicles have been GM cars, in large part because those were the cars I grew up with. In addition to the numerous used/beater Cutlasses, Regals, Bonnevilles, Cutlass Cruisers and Le Sabres, my parents' first brand new automobile purchase was a brown 1984 Chevrolet Cavalier sedan. Moreover, I passed my driving test in an '86 Cavalier. Naturally, for me this started a fascination with J-cars that I had to quench at least three times.

Okay…confession time. Here is something I've never told anyone until now. I am embarrassed to say that when I was young, aside from the fact that I secretly liked some (not all) songs by The New Kids on the Block, I also drank the Kool Aid regarding the Cadillac Cimarron. Namely, that the Cimarron and by extension, all the J-cars—Cavalier, Firenza, Skyhawk, and Sunbird—were sports sedans. There, I said it. What's more, I believed that my J-cars, all stock with at best the 2-liter pushrod four, were the equal of my cousin's '88 Plymouth Conquest TSI Turbo. Ah…the foolishness of youth!

CIMARRON vs CAVALIER

After the '81 Skylark from last week's COAL, bit the dust, I replaced it with an '85 Chevy Cavalier station wagon, in metallic blue. The car had a dented left rear passenger door with some rust starting at the bottom. This was the only aesthetic imperfection. The car had the base 2.0 liter, four-cylinder engine rated at an optimistic 90 HP and had no options except the three-speed automatic transmission and a rear defroster. It did not have air conditioning.

However, compared with the "broughamness" of my Skylark, the Cavalier was European and sporty. In my eyes it came very close to my friend's brand new Corsica. A deal was struck with the owner, a woman named Georgetta, and the car, which we subsequently also named Georgetta, came home with us.

http://www.curbsideclassic.com/wp-content/uploads/2014/10/1983-Chevrolet-Chevy-Cavalier-Cadet-Station-Wagon-CS-Fuel-Injection-Buick-Skyhawk-Cadillac-Cimarron-Oldsmobile-Firenza-Pontiac-Sunbird-Vauxhall-Isuzu-Aska-Holden-Camira-5-Door-5-speed-manual-3-speed-automatic-transmission.jpg

Georgetta actually served us well. Its station wagon body with rear door and extra cargo space proved very useful to us. In time however, a few problems developed. First, one of the mounts for the driver's seat came loose. This caused some interesting dynamics for whomever was driving the car. Upon acceleration or turning, the driver would at best hear a sudden squeaking noise and at worst the seat would pivot forward diagonally. You would eventually get used to it but it could be very annoying and disconcerting.

One day, as I was driving down the same steep hill where my **Buick Century** met its end, I looked down to see the red brake-warning light illuminated! You can imagine my fear that history would repeat itself with a head-on collision with a light pole. Except this time I would not be in a large six- passenger sedan but a small subcompact wagon. Thankfully, the brakes were just fine, and it quickly became evident that there was some kind of electrical issue causing the brake light to come on.

I could not stand driving it with that red light on so I took it to an "automotive electrician" — big mistake. When I got the car back, not only was the brake warning light still on but now the check engine light was on as well. This is where I learned one of my few automotive skills, the art of using black electrical tape to cover up annoying warning lights. By this time, the car would also make a strange burping and gurgling sound after shutting down after a long drive. These things, along with the lack of A/C, made me grow tired of Georgetta and I readily agreed to giving it to my Dad, who was essentially looking for a "work truck" in exchange for another vehicle.

That vehicle was a white 1984 Chevrolet Cavalier sedan. This time it was a CS or more luxury-trimmed model. The upholstery was a bit better; in addition to automatic transmission, it also had cruise and intermittent wipers, plus the factory cassette player had auto reverse and Dolby noise reduction.

The powerplant was the same 2-liter found in Georgetta. An issue was the car's white paint, which was peeling and in terrible shape. What to do? In those days black cars, instead of being ubiquitous, were considered mysterious, cool, and sporty. I took the car to one of those $99 paint job places (do they exist anymore?) and asked them to paint it black. There were two problems: 1) They didn't have black, and 2) It would cost much more to paint the car because the previous imperfections of the old paint would have to be removed in order for the new paint to adhere properly. My solution. 1) No black? No problem. Paint it the darkest shade of blue you can find 2) As for the imperfections...just paint over them...I'll take my chances. After signing numerous disclaimers they agreed to paint the car and I got my black (er...midnight blue) sports sedan.

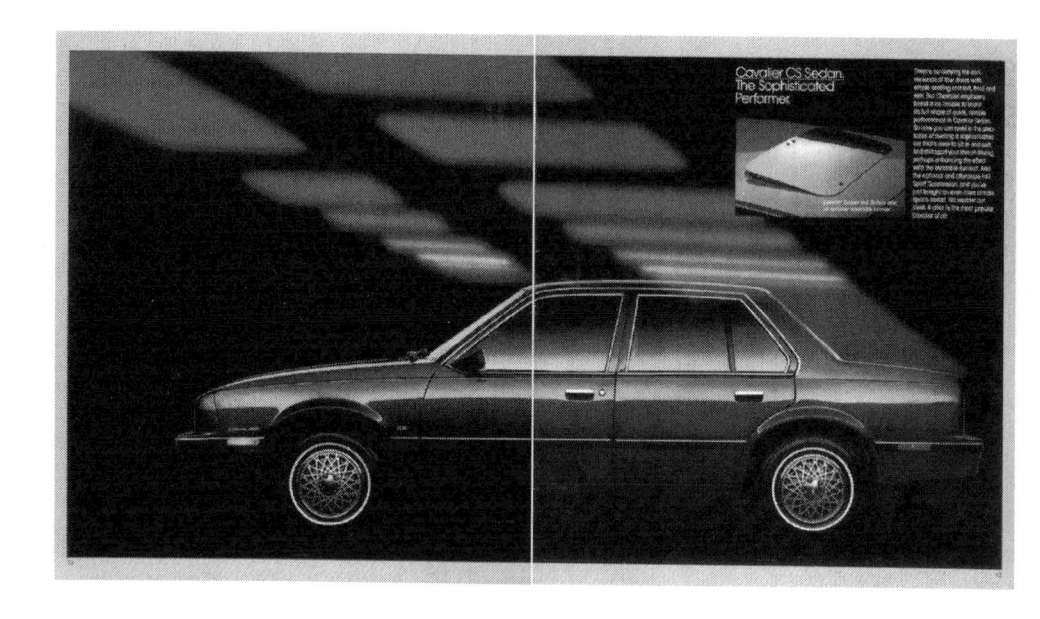

Despite the horrible paint job, I enjoyed living my delusion for a short time until the head gasket went, causing coolant contamination in the oil and rapid loss of compression. I still remember the sick feeling I had when I pulled the dipstick and was presented with the creamy, milky, goop that was coolant mixed with oil.

I soon began to complain about a radical loss of power, so my Mom asked to take the car to work one day to see if it was my imagination or if something really was amiss. To this day, almost 25 years later, she still maintains that was the worst and scariest car that she has ever driven. Two subsequent attempts to rebuild the engine ended in failure, and we eventually sold it and the Georgetta wagon to some auto tinkerers looking for cheap wheels. I think they gave us $300 for both cars.

Meanwhile, my Mom had a beige 53,000 mile '84 Pontiac Sunbird wagon that I really wanted. My chance came when she said that she was looking for something sportier. I offered to help her find her new ride as long as I could have the Sunbird when she was done with it. After looking at a Mustang, a Camaro, and a 280 ZX, she eventually settled for a two-door Mazda 626 which left me we with the Sunbird "sports wagon."

In my **previous COAL**, I mentioned that the Skylark looked like a smaller Regal. Well in this case, I thought the front of the Sunbird was made to look like a smaller Firebird.

Plus, the instrument panel lit up in red at night…just like a BMW! It even had an exotic engine…a 1.8-liter. This engine, sourced from GM of Brazil, is apparently still produced today. A turbo version, rated at 165 HP, was produced for the Sunbird but mine had the naturally aspirated version, rated at 85 HP. The badge on the fender read "OHC/FI"…just like a Honda Prelude (right)! In my mind I had a combination Firebird, BMW, and Prelude…plus it was a station wagon…perfection itself! My own "pocket rocket." Again, the ignorance and foolishness of youth.

I began to "modify" it to fit in with my vision of it being a "sports wagon." I tinted the glass, upgraded the sound system, and attached red "sporty-looking" stripes to it.

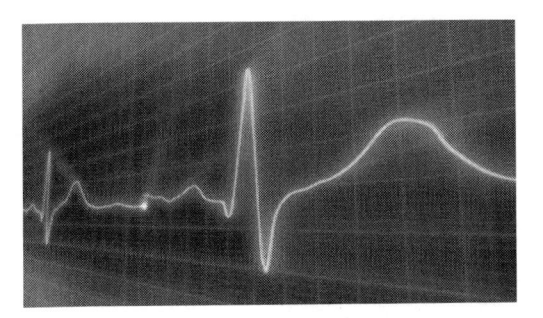

I even attached stickers that looked like pulses from an EKG meter (still highly embarrassed by this).

In addition, I had the timing advanced in an effort to improve acceleration. This was also the era when all kinds of fuel and oil additives were being sold claiming to improve vehicle performance. I fell for it, hook, line and sinker, and dumped them all into that vehicle.

Actually, that car served me pretty well. It was reliable and got me through most of college. I have fond memories of it being versatile, fun and, yes, reasonably sporty. The car endured so many indignities and downright abuse from yours truly, including regular "speed runs" to bury the needle of its 85 MPH speedometer, neutral drops at least once a week, a few off road excursions, and my attempts on the Garden State Parkway at imitating Cole Trickle from the newly released film *Days of Thunder*.

My Dad's 1982 Pontiac Bonneville wagon had gone to its eternal reward, so my Dad needed another "work truck" again. After helping me move into my dorm room one more time, my Dad took over the Sunbird for another couple of years or so until it eventually died a natural death when the engine gave out after a little over 100,000 miles.

Cured of my J-body obsession for now (there would be more later), <u>its replacement, which I'll talk about next time, was a bit</u>

more crude and primitive.

1976 Chevrolet Camaro – "A Quick Fling on the Wild Side"

So my Mom's co-worker's son, Nick, had just graduated from grad school and scored a job as a chemist at a large pharmaceutical company. Since Nick was a young unmarried guy, the first thing he did with his fat paycheck was upgrade his wheels.

Being a fan of muscle cars, he bought the contemporary equivalent of a new muscle car, a 1991 Oldsmobile Calais 442 with the famous Quad 4 engine.

This left him the question of what to do with his old ride, a 1976 Camaro. Since his Mom and my Mom were not only co-workers but friends, she convinced Nick to give me the car. On my end, there was no problem with the idea of a free Camaro.

My first thought when we got to their house upon seeing the Camaro was how much it dwarfed Nick's new "muscle car." It was obvious which car had the V8 and which one was a four-banger. I must say that the 442 did look pretty good in its shiny new black paint. My second thought was how ugly the Camaro looked. However, instead of being repulsed by its ugliness I actually found myself attracted to it. It wasn't the type of ugly that left you disgusted, but so ugly that it was at once intimidating and strangely compelling.

This picture from the internet does not quite do the actual car justice. The body was much rougher than depicted above. It was originally silver which had faded to a very dull gray–so faded that when I first saw it, I thought that it was unpainted dull metal. There was rust rot in the lower rear quarters and sections where there were no lower rear quarters, just holes where the rust had eaten through. There were a few bondo patches, and the wheels were bare steelies with no hub caps.

The interior was austere and in poor condition. The headliner had been removed a long time ago; the black vinyl seats were torn and covered with very poor fitting seat covers; the automatic transmission lever had no shift boot cover, so you could see down into its inner workings; and all the weatherstripping had grown very brittle, so the interior leaked when it rained. It sat low–much lower than my Pontiac Sunbird, and lower than Nick's 442. It sat in the street, a bold, imposing presence in the neighborhood.

As our parents began to socialize, Nick gave me an orientation to the car. I remember the first thing he said to me: "Just so you know, this car beat a Monte Carlo SS on the Garden State Parkway doing 130 mph." "O…kay" I said. He responded, " I just wanted to make sure you knew what the car can do."

The car was a base Camaro with a few options. While it did not have the rear spoiler common to so many of these cars, it did have the 350 V8 engine, smog-restricted to 165 HP with torque listed at 260 lb. ft. at 2400 RPM. The car had no inside hood release. One gained access to the engine compartment through a hidden lever in the front of the car. There was no rear defroster.

While the car came with factory air, Nick said that it had been disconnected long ago. In addition, while the blower fan was operable the heat was on all the time with no way to restrict it from coming into the cabin. The high-beam switch was mounted on the floor by the brake pedal, which I thought was kinda neat. Also, the ignition lock was broken so the car could be started without the key, and the windows struggled to stay in the up position.

The car's aura was what the early Dodge Vipers wanted to capture. A primitive, crude, rude, bare-bones beast of a sports car that was unapologetic and imposing. Its one concession to comfort was an Alpine removable face cassette player (remember those?). One concern was that at 158,000 miles the car had extremely high mileage (for the time). Nick's response was "these engines only get better with age." Besides, the car was being given to me free of charge so the mileage issue was quickly forgotten.

In order to start the car, one had to follow a special starting procedure which I cannot now remember, but which involved some combination of pumping, half pumping, turning, and half turning and pumping again. It was complicated, but it served as an effective anti theft system since the windows would not stay up and the car could be started without the ignition key. The exhaust was rotten, which made the sound from the 350 V8 much more noticeable.

One more thing—the trunk was jammed shut, but you could open it by using the Fonz's method of banging it just so and it would pop open like magic. I never mastered the trunk-opening technique. It worked sometimes but not always.

It was just as well, since the trunk was no longer watertight and as a result was quite nasty. Needless to say, I never used the trunk. In fact, I remember helping my dad with a fence project and having to haul multiple 60 pound bags of cement in the back seat of the Camaro.

It reminded me very much of an F15 Eagle Fighter jet. Big, gray, imposing, and all business with impressive off the line thrust. The car was very different from the front-drive GM A and X cars and J cars I was familiar with.

I did enjoy the car. The torque was very noticeable when accelerating and I clearly remember beating a Mustang in a side-by-side race up a steep hill. With it's low driving position, stiff suspension, uncomfortable seats and lack of creature comforts, the car was not easy to drive, but was fun on a nice day and definitely stood out from the crowd. I particularly liked (and still do) accelerating away from toll booths. It gave me such a rush!

On early Sunday mornings, I would take it to South Mountain Reservation with its twisty roads and uphill S-turns in order to enjoy the car. Many times, I just enjoyed opening the hood and admiring the engine. I really enjoyed the fact that it had no computer, so no pesky Check Engine lights that drove me crazy in my last vehicles. Also, unlike my previous vehicles, it was actually very reliable, not stranding me or requiring any repairs in the ten months or so that I owned it.

The fun came to an end for several reasons. Winter was coming and the car had wide summer tires, not good in a rear-wheel-drive V8-powered car with a light rear end. Plus, the windows would not stay up and the weatherstripping was worn. In addition, according to Nick it was known to not start reliably in winter. Most importantly, the frame had quite a bit of rot to it so it was becoming unsafe. We reluctantly had it towed to the scrapyard before the heavy snow started. But it was fun while it lasted. I just realized that this is the last two-door vehicle I have owned.

It was replaced by a distant relative that had many of its attributes but was much more practical. **I will talk about that one next time.**

1978 Chevrolet Caprice Classic – "Coming of Age Car"

By the time of my last year in college and the beginning of my grad school career, I had experienced a wide range of automobiles. On one end, I had my **76 Camaro;** on the other end, I had my **J Cars**; and in the middle, my **Buick Century and Skylark**.

My next choice of vehicle was influenced by the V8 power of my Camaro, the cargo room and versatility of my J-body wagons, and the comfort of my Buicks. The numerous commercials for the Lexus LS 400 and Infiniti Q45 also made me look to large, V8 powered sedans for their smoothness and power.

In addition, the TV show *Cops* was in its heyday as was *Real Stories of the Highway Patrol*. Every week, I saw the Chevy Caprice in action. I saw a powerful, rugged vehicle that could go anywhere and endure all kinds of abuse. In addition, I saw all the equipment that could be crammed into them and had an appreciation for how roomy they were. I immediately let it be known to all that I was in the market for a Caprice. My friends and family helped with the search but a few misunderstood me. They thought I was looking for a Capri (as in Mercury Capri); I had to clarify more than a few times that it was a Caprice that I wanted.

A few weeks later, I was awakened by an early phone call from my Dad. In his travels, he had run across an estate sale—and lo and behold, there was a 1978 Caprice Classic in the driveway for sale with 50,000 one-owner miles. Needless to say, I got out of bed and hightailed it over there.

The car was indeed a one-owner (recently deceased), low mileage original in a two-tone dark and light blue combination, just sitting in the driveway. The first picture in this post is a twin of the actual car. My jaw dropped when I first saw it…I thought I was seeing a ghost! The asking price was $700, but I had Dad and his negotiation skills with me that day, which allowed me to leave with the car for $500.

Despite the low mileage, the car was not in mint condition. I suspect this was primarily because it had been stored outside most of its life. The paint was faded, as was the powder blue, button-tufted interior, and the dash pad was cracked from exposure to the sun. The equipment told me a little about the former owner's priorities. The car had air conditioning, a rear defroster, and power windows and locks, my first car to be so equipped, I was so excited! However, it did not have cruise control and only had an AM Radio with just one speaker in the center of the dash! I thought that the windshield-integrated antenna was kind of neat.

What really closed the deal for me was that the engine was basically the same 5.7 liter 350 V8 found in myCamaro. I subsequently tested its prowess a few times in the Caprice through the impromptu drag races of youth, when I beat an '87 Camaro, '84 Dodge Daytona and '90 Mitsubishi Eclipse.

**THE NEW CHEVROLET
1978 Caprice Classic and Impala.**

The car was huge compared to my friends' newer cars at the time. Its capacity for people and cargo made it a popular vehicle for our outings or when a friend needed help moving. I routinely used the full capacity of its six-passenger seating and occasionally exceeded it. Using bungee cords allowed all manner of items to be placed in its enormous trunk, including a filing cabinet, a small couch, and a refrigerator. Folks began referring to it as a truck due to its size and versatility. It certainly had presence. I loved the wide expanse of hood from the driver's seat and the way it dwarfed the other cars around it. I usually had club music or the theme from *Cops* blaring out the window "Bad boys, Bad boys…what you gonna do when they come for you!" The V8 engine was so smooth and gave a satisfying hum when pushed.

Until the radical restyling in '91, you can trace its evolution from its '75-'76 predecessor just by studying the front end;

1976

1978 (the 77's had a slightly different grille)

1980

1986

1987

1991

I absolutely love the big grille and wide stance! You can trace the look all the way back to '76.

2012

The latest Caprice looks very different. It still looks pretty rugged, though.

Anyway, getting back to my '78; In the wintertime, I thought it's rear-wheel-drive setup would be a problem but it really wasn't that bad. I passed many a redesigned round Caprice or Roadmaster stuck in the snow spinning its wheels. In fact, a South Orange, NJ police officer whose department just transitioned to the round Caprices remarked "that's a better Chevy than the new ones since they're not so light in the back." Not that the car was as good as my previous front-wheel-drive vehicles. There were several times accelerating or turning in the wet when I was reminded which end was doing the driving and had to wrestle with the car to point it in the right direction.

THE BLIZZARD OF 1996
JAN 6-9, 1996
SNOWFALL (INCHES)
30+
20-30
10-20
Boston 19"
New York City 21"
Philadelphia 31"
Baltimore 27"
Washington, D.C. 20"
©2003 ACCUWEATHER, INC.   WEB: WWW.ACCUWEATHER.COM   EMAIL: INFO@ACCUWEATHER.COM

One of those occasions was the infamous blizzard of '96 that effectively shut down New Jersey. I had to go to a funeral that week. It was like driving in the North Pole. You couldn't see the road, let alone the lanes. Everything was covered with layers of snow. There were quite a few close calls when I skidded right through red lights. White-knuckle driving all the way. Believe it or not, the Caprice got me there and back. I was stuck just once, but got out of the way just in time to avoid being creamed by a fire truck.

PANORAMIC Rearview Mirror
- Fits Over Any Existing Mirror
- Distortion Free Glass
- Ideal for All Vehicles
Prevents Accidents
Wide Angle View
ELIMINATE BLIND SPOTS!

I replaced the stock AM radio with a Sony cassette head unit and added two speakers in the rear parcel shelf to supplement the lone speaker in the dashboard. I compensated for the lack of dual side mirrors with a huge panoramic rear view mirror. To this day, the best rear view mirror I've ever had–literally getting rid of all the blind spots and eliminating the need for side view mirrors altogether. Unfortunately, there was one unintended "modification." A few nights after I got it, my sister accidentally backed into the driver's side with my old Sunbird. The damage was actually quite minor but my attempts at repair worsened it as I banged the dent out too much so that it bubbled out. The inside door panel was never quite the same after my "repair."

The car did begin to show its age under my ownership. The AC and power locks stopped working, the radiator and water pump needed to be replaced, the carburetor needed to be rebuilt and the windshield wiper motor failed. I remember having to limp home from Grandma's house with a damaged master cylinder. It was a very tense 45 miles with only half the brake system operating. These repairs were not cheap (for a first-year grad student, at least). I never did fix the AC or power locks. I remember having to borrow money from my school for the funds to keep it going.

LAKE ERIE
OHIO'S GREAT LAKE

This is the car that I think of when I reminisce about my college road trips. A particularly memorable one was when we decided one night to see how far we could drive in eight hours in a randomly selected direction. The direction chosen was west, so we ended up driving 500 miles from South Orange, NJ, leaving at 10 pm and arriving and having breakfast at the shores of Lake Erie, in Ohio, eight hours later– and then turning around to return to NJ shortly after. That was one of the many times when I wished I had a camera!

On the trip back, I was impressed with the V8 engine's performance as we kept pace with a Jaguar XJ6 through the mountains of Pennsylvania, with the speedometer pinned beyond its 80 mph limit for well over two hours. We ended the chase only because we ran low on fuel. The mountainous terrain and our high speed meant about four refueling stops. We were back in New Jersey in time for dinner, with some great stories to tell our friends.

It is hard to put into words my feelings toward this car...I loved it! When I think of the friendships and good times of my youth, this is the car I associate with them. It was the ultimate road trip mobile!

Why did I part ways with this car? One reason was that I was continuing my graduate studies in Baltimore and wanted something newer, trimmer and more fuel efficient. The second reason is that a good friend of mine who loved the car as much as I did (her previous ride was a C-series pickup) was graduating and needed a car for work. As much as I loved the car, I loved our friendship more. So, I promised her the car as soon as she secured a parking spot for it, a few weeks after her graduation.

Here is a funny postscript to this story: As reliable as the car was, the day she and her boyfriend came to get it was the only time it didn't start! The car refused to leave my side! No amount of pumping or jump starting would wake the Chevy from its slumber. What finally worked? A command from its new owner. She told her boyfriend to pour fuel down the carb. He was terrified and I grabbed the fire extinguisher. She got behind the wheel, held down the accelerator and turned the key, and the car miraculously roared to life under new ownership. It was a bittersweet feeling watching her drive away in the car I loved the most.

The car served her well. She took it on many

more road trips and adventures, including a run-in with a new BMW. The Bimmer had to be towed from the scene, while the Caprice suffered only a badly mangled license plate. She kept the car until the early 2000s, when it finally wore out and was traded in for her first brand new car.

As for me, I replaced the Caprice with something much different that was a bridge to a new chapter in my life. I'll discuss that one next time. And don't worry, there are seven more B-body vehicles to discuss further in this series, so stay tuned!

1986 Pontiac Grand Am – "We Build Excitement…In Baltimore"

I had just given away the best car that I had ever owned to this point. Why? Because I was leaving for grad school in Baltimore, 180 miles away, and my car was getting close to 20 years old (ancient in those days), plus I was looking for something newer and more fuel efficient. I had a small stipend given to me by the organization sending me to grad school which I used to purchase my next vehicle.

Thar car turned out to be a 1986 Pontiac Grand Am sedan with about 55,000 miles on it. It was a boring/ugly shade of brownish gold with a crack in the windshield.

And under the hood…my old friend the 2.5 liter Iron Duke rated at 92 horsepower. The car looked just like the picture above except it had four doors. In researching this article, I found that there are very few pictures of the '85-'91 four door Grand Ams available online. Especially the early ones with the sealed beam headlights.

Along with the Buick Somerset and Olds Calais, the Pontiac Grand Am was built on the N body platform intended to replace the X body which was sold until 1985. The Grand Am was marketed as a sporty car for the 80's yuppie set. Chevy's X body replacements were the similar L bodies consisting of the Corsica and Berreta.

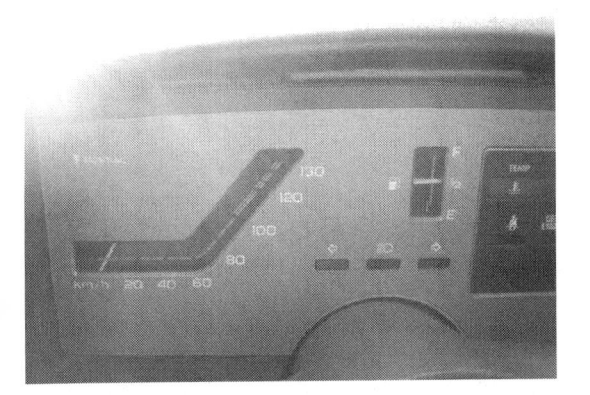

Despite the car's "sporty" evident..in an starters it had looking dash brown color, the theme was 80's sort of way. For a tacky digital mimicking actual digital dashes of the day. Light and wiper controls were also pod mounted which was considered high tech back then.

The seats were also patterned after small sport sedans. The interior contained absolutely no wood trim or living room easy chair seating. There were even headrests for the rear seat passengers, unusual for the GM cars of the day. Another novelty was that the power window switches were on the console, another nod to "sport sedans."

Before my big move to Baltimore, a few repairs and modifications were undertaken. The cracked windshield was replaced as well as a headlight switch which melted shortly after getting the car. I remember going to the parts store and requesting one. They only had switches for the '73-'75 Grand Ams available! My part had to be ordered. This is when I learned that the Grand Am name **predated 1985**. We also replaced the stock AM/FM radio with a head unit with a cassette player. The previous owner said the AC "just needed a charge." He was right, after getting it charged it was blowing ice cold. I'm sure I don't have to say it but...of course, in a few months it needed another charge as it was no longer blowing ice cold.

Anyway, I packed the car, which was actually a lot roomier than it looked, and headed down to school. My parents followed me with the rest of my stuff in my Mom's newest J car, a Buick Skyhawk two door sedan, and helped me move into my new school in the Roland Park section of Baltimore.

While at school, I had an internship twice a week about 5 or 6 miles away. So having a car was advantageous. In my free time, it also took me shopping, dining, and socializing. In addition, it also allowed me to go home to New Jersey whenever I wanted. The car was very good on gas and was not bad in terms of performance. It did not have the off the line torque of my Caprice or Camaro but could keep up with traffic reasonably well. Acceleration was more than adequate with a little bit of torque steer. That is, once you hit 80 or so, after that, the steering wheel began to vibrate and the engine noise approached motorcycle levels serving as a warning that you were nearing the limits of its performance envelope. It did handle pretty well and its trim dimensions inspired confidence in tight spaces and emergency maneuvers.

I was lonely and homesick in Baltimore but not for long. At my internship I met the young woman who would eventually become my wife. The car took us on our early dates and also provided us with privacy since neither of our living situations at the time afforded us much alone time. We spent many hours in that car taking it all over Maryland. I remember it as comfortable, quick, and versatile and also quite economical. This was important because I left school at the end of that year and began looking for a job. The car was great there too, taking me to my many job interviews.

Because I was out of school, I needed a place to live. Because I wanted to be close to my girl, I looked for a job in Baltimore. That search took a few months which left me essentially homeless in the meantime. I alternated between staying at Mom and Dad's, Motel Rooms, friends' couches, and yes, one or two nights in the Grand Am at various rest stops. Thankfully, I found gainful employment by the end of the summer and moved into an apartment in early September.

When the car hit 68,000 miles, the Check Engine Light came on. This was not unfamiliar to me. Like the Iron Duke engine in my **Skylark and Century**, it came equipped with an early version of GM's Computer Command Control (CCC) for the emissions system. Like my Skylark, the CEL illuminated around 68,000 miles and would go on or off intermittently despite attempts by many to clear/read/resolve the trouble code. It was determined that in order to really fix it, I would need a new CCC which everyone (including the mechanics) believed to be a waste of time and money. While this problem was annoying, the worst was yet to come.

It started with an oil spot. I checked my oil, it was a little low so I topped it off. The next time I returned home to New Jersey I had my mechanic take care of the oil leak. No problem, leak fixed, no more oil spots…for about a month.

Then the oil spots returned. A few small spots at first, eventually worsening until the spots it left looked like the picture above. The place I worked for was located in a residential neighborhood in Towson, Maryland. There was no parking lot by my office so I parked in front of the house across the street. I remember how embarrased I felt when the owner of that house came into my office and begged me not to park there anymore because I was ruining his curb appeal...he was absolutely right.

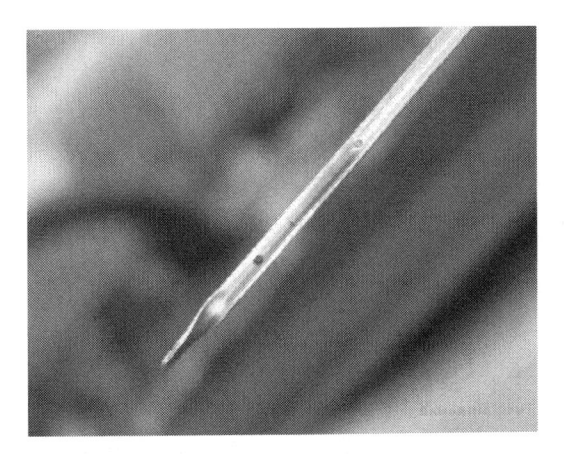

I found it puzzling that despite the massive environmental disaster I was creating, the dipstick registered full. It was leaking like crazy, yet the crankcase always showed full.

To this day, I don't know how I could have overlooked what the problem was. It became crystal clear one day on York Road when a huge amount of smoke began pouring out from underneath the car and the car was barely crawling forward. What an idiot I was...the oil leaking out was not motor oil...it was transmission oil! The entire time that the car was leaking, I never bothered to crawl underneath to see what kind of fluid was leaking...I just assumed that it was motor oil. Because of my stupidity/laziness, all the trans oil was now gone so the transmission was cooking itself! I pulled into a gas station, bought a few bottles of ATF, and believe it or not, the transmission was fine. In addition, despite **my past experiences with the 2.5 liter Iron Duke,** the one in the Grand Am continued to run strong and reliably.

That's pretty much how I rolled for the next few months, I'd fill it up with trans fluid and it would be good for about two weeks. Of course the two weeks, became one week, the one week became....you get the picture. Towards the end, my trunk had a case of ATF at all times. It was especially awkward when I drove people around and had to pull over abruptly to pour fluid in. I recall a trip back from New Jersey when I had to pull over about eight times to top it off. I'm still amazed that the transmission itself did not fail. By the way, my mechanic confirmed that one of the main seals was compromised and the cost to fix the problem was far more than I could afford.

With no money, a new life in Baltimore, and the necessity of a car, **I needed a solution. This will be the subject of my next COAL.**

"Pentastar Partners – Short Timers"

This COAL is dedicated to my parents, who got me through some tough times

Act 1: 1985 Chrysler LeBaron-Surprise Attack

So my Grand Am could carry me no longer. I was starting a new life in Baltimore with a job that necessitated a car. I was also broke. It was the goodness of my parents that got me out of this mess.

My Dad liked to keep random extra cars around. "In case someone needs it." He would say. Whenever I visited, there was always a random surprise in the driveway. The "special guest cars" varied wildly from a Ford Fairmont to a Dodge Shadow, to a Ford Escort, to an Oldsmobile Cutlass, to a Mercedes W126. I could easily do a separate COAL series on the surprises I found in my parent's driveway. Up until the mid 90's Dad's daily drivers were almost always GM cars. His extra cars were always something different.

This time Dad's extra car was a 1985 Chrysler LeBaron with 120,000 well cared for miles. Dad had acquired it from an elderly first owner. It was mine to use no questions asked…thanks Dad!

Despite its mini limousine looks, this generation LeBaron was just a Dodge Aries with a fancy suit. Fake wood, and living room interior fittings abounded. The car was a light blue with blue cloth interior that was in very good shape.

During this time in my life, I was constantly traveling back and fourth from New Jersey to Maryland. The car came equipped with the 2.2 liter four cylinder rated at 99 horsepower. While not a fast car, I remember the car being comfortable and competent on the highway. The other thing I remember is the optical illusion that the styling produced. Those around me thought I was driving a large car. Someone referred to it as "an old boat."

Although it certainly did have all the styling cues of the big Chryslers of the past, my <u>Grand Am</u> was around the same size if not bigger, and nobody ever referred to it as a "boat." I wish those people had seen my <u>Caprice</u>. If the LeBaron was a "boat" to them, then the <u>Caprice</u> was an aircraft carrier! But I digress. The LeBaron provided me with comfortable and reliable transportation for about a month.

One day, when I was on my way to work, I stopped at a gas station to fill up. I was sitting in the car when I heard "give me the f****** money!" I then heard angry voices and then a scuffle. Something told me to get down. I found myself in the middle of a gas station robbery. The next second, I felt a sudden jolting impact and was thrown forward. I looked up in time to see the rear end of a silver Mazda 626 escaping from the gas station.

My heart sank when I stepped out of the car to see that the entire rear end of my car was destroyed by the fleeing getaway car. The red taillight lenses lay shattered on the ground and all the taillight bulbs were visible. The rear quarters were deformed which caused the trunk lid to deform upwards in the middle so that you could peer into the interior of the trunk. How that 626 did this much damage to my car and still managed to escape under its own power is still a mystery.

Both our insurance company and the insurance company of the gas station gave us a hard time about compensating us for the damage with each side claiming that the other was responsible for compensation. Meanwhile, I had to get to work. My understanding and patient Dad helped me to temporarily make the car legal to drive by putting some clear red lens repair tape over the exposed tail light bulbs. Despite being smashed in the back, the car seemed unfazed and continued to provide me with reliable transportation for the next few months.

Act 2 1987 Chrysler New Yorker Turbo-History Repeats Itself

I continued to drive the battered LeBaron until Mom got herself a brand new Honda Civic. Seeing my need, she gave me her now surplus white 1987 Chrysler New Yorker Turbo. Like the LeBaron, it was basically a Dodge Aries but it had a few tricks up its sleeve.

The New Yorker Turbo was the flagship of the Chrysler lineup in 1987. It was equipped with a 146 horsepower turbocharged four cylinder that contemporary media claimed " had the acceleration of a V8."

The interior had the luxury living room treatment with the blue poofy velour seats and wood galore.

The car also had all electronic instruments, power everything, automatic climate control (inoperative), overhead console with external temperature display (also inoperative) and the *Knight Rider* inspired Voice Alert warning system. A robotic male voice intoned "please fasten your seat belt." When you did, he would actually say, "thank you." He said other things too: "lights are on," "there is a door ajar," "all systems are normal." There was something wrong with the digital speedometer. When you first started out, the display was blank. You could not tell how fast you were going.

It took about 15 minutes for it to kick in and the display would light up and everything would be normal. It kinda reminded me of the old tube TVs where there was a delay between switching it on and actually being able to see something. The turbo produced a high pitch whine similar to a siren but did provide pretty good acceleration.

**The New Chrysler New Yorker.
Turbo-charged power. Front-wheel drive.
Even when you're sitting in the lap of luxury,
you're still in the driver's seat.**

The moment you enter your Chrysler New Yorker you enter a world of luxury.
A world of inner quiet that shields you from blaring city noise. Power and convenience systems that instill a strong sense of command.
But New Yorker's luxury extends far beyond comforts and conveniences. Chrysler believes a luxury car should also be an incredible driving car.
That's why New Yorker's advanced front-wheel drive and positive-response suspension are designed to give agility and control. You can sail into a turn with confidence.
That's why New Yorker

offers you the option of turbopower.
And whether you buy or lease, New Yorker gives you the luxury of a 5-year or 50,000-mile Protection Plan.* Even your turbo is covered.
New Yorker. Luxury that has kept pace with the technology of driving. Because even when you're sitting in the lap of luxury, Chrysler wants you to be in the driver's seat.
Test drive New Yorker at your Chrysler-Plymouth dealer. Buckle up for safety.
Chrysler. Driving to be the best.

Chrysler Motors
Best built, best backed American cars and trucks.

Chrysler
Division of Chrysler Motors

Full of gratitude, I took the car back to my place in Baltimore. A few days later, My future wife and I went out to dinner with a friend of mine. At dinner my friend was recounting to us how her son had borrowed her Corolla and gotten into an accident with it and found a cheap body shop in the area and gotten it repaired better than new. " What a nice boy," we said and continued a lovely evening with friends. Little did we know, that we would be calling on that cheap body shop less than 12 hours later.

The next morning I was driving to work. My route that morning took me through horse country in Northern Baltimore County. It was a beautiful Fall day and I was listening to some nice smooth jazz on the high end aftermarket stereo Dad had installed as a gift for Mom. It was really a gorgeous day with beautiful scenery. I'm not really sure what happened next. I remember the car wandering slightly onto the shoulder and when I tried to correct it, the car spun around 360 degrees a few times. The car busted through a farm fence. Through the windshield, I saw horses scattering out of the way just a few feet from my out of control car.

The car came to rest in a ditch in a pasture in the middle of a horse farm. The front bumper was sheared off, both fenders were mangled and both front doors opened and closed funny. Extremely embarrassed, I called my friend who had hosted us for dinner the previous night and had to sheepishly ask, "Uh, whats the name of that body shop again?" We took it to that shop and after evaluating the damage for ten minutes, they looked at me and sadly shook their heads saying that it would not be an easy nor practical fix.

My next call was tougher still. I had to call my parents and tell them that I had totaled the second car they lent me to replace the previous car they had lent me which I had also totaled. Their kindness amazed me when they reimbursed the farmer whose fence I had broken and whose peaceful horse farm I had intruded upon.

With no other choice, I continued to drive it like that for a while. Like the LeBaron, it proved quite operable despite the heavy damage. Although occasionally the *Knight Rider* system would say "your door is ajar" when it was not actually the case. However, before long, the transmission began to slip. In a cruel repeat of the fates of both the LeBaron and my previous Pontiac Grand Am, I realized that the New Yorker's transaxle was damaged by the impact and the car would soon be immobile.

So I was once again in need of a car. <u>My next COAL would be my first foray into foreign territory.</u>

1983 Saab – "My SAAB Story"

This COAL is dedicated to my Mom who was there for me through this ordeal.

 It was the Spring of 1998, my <u>Grad School career</u> had abruptly ended a year earlier. I found a job working for a small company for not much more than minimum wage. Money was tight and my automotive luck had run out. My 1986 <u>Pontiac Grand Am</u> had just suffered transmission failure. The loaner <u>Chrysler LeBaron</u> from my Dad's fleet was <u>severely damaged</u> in a hit and run. My Mom was generous enough to lend me her <u>1987 Chrysler New Yorker Turbo</u>. Unfortunately, the New Yorker was <u>totaled</u> in a one car accident a week after she had loaned it to me. I was utterly humiliated!

I thought I had hit the lowest point possible. I had no more than $400, zero mechanical skills, and needed a car for work. With the world wide web relatively new, I relied on *Auto Trader* to help me find my next vehicle. Due to my limited funds I had three options:

Option 1: Two 1981 Ford Thunderbirds. Neither vehicle was running but the seller guaranteed that I could make one operable vehicle out of the two hulks.

Option 2: 1980 Dodge St. Regis. I so wanted this car. It was brown and seemed relatively straight. However, the owner assured me that although it ran and drove it would never pass Maryland State Inspection in part because it had no exhaust system and for other reasons that he did not really want to get into.

Option 3: 1983 Saab 900 sedan. Ran and drove with 180,000 miles dealer serviced. I called the seller who told me that it was her daughter's daily driver. While she could not guarantee that the car would pass inspection, there was no reason for it not to since it was driven daily by her daughter.

I really wanted the St. Regis but needed something that would pass inspection because I needed a car for work. The two Thunderbirds sounded intriguing but I had zero mechanical skills, space, or money to tackle such a project. At the time, it seemed like the Saab was the logical choice so I called the seller to make the appointment.

I showed up there with my girlfriend (who would eventually become my wife) expecting an ugly rusted eyesore of a car but was very pleasantly surprised. As far as I know, the above is not a picture of the actual car but it looked identical to this picture I took from the Internet. The fact that we lived in Maryland and the pictured car has D.C. plates makes me wonder if it's the same car.

The car was a base non turbo model with the 2 liter four cylinder model with 116 HP. The only "luxury" features on the car were air conditioning, automatic transmission, cruise control – which I never used – and an aftermarket tape deck which funnily enough, was the same unit that came with my '76 Camaro. Small world, I guess.

I immediately fell in love with its styling and European flavor after having only owned American cars. I liked the full set of gauges and especially liked the novelty of the ignition key in the center console which was a Saab hallmark at the time. The AC blew ice cold, the car started right up and sounded strong, there was a new oil change sticker, and there were no dents and very, very little rust. The interior was spotless except for a slightly sagging headliner. To top it off, I loved the folding rear seat, something none of my previous sedans had before. Little did I know how handy it would come in later.

The seller gave us the keys and told us to drive for as long as we wanted to, so the two of us got in the car and drove it for a good hour. The car accelerated well with no strange sounds. It was the first car I had driven with four wheel disc brakes so I was amazed at its stopping ability. Everything was great until the very end of the test drive when we heard a hissing noise. At first I thought flat tire or other mechanical failure until I looked at my girlfriend who seemed so much shorter all of a sudden. Apparently, her seat bottom had broken and she was now practically sitting on the floor! No problem I said, we'll just get some throw pillows to boost the seat back up. If this was the only problem with this "exotic" car, to me, it was still a bargain.

So we want back to the seller who unexpectedly took $50 off the price of the car with one proviso: once we took possession of the title, we were to take the car, and never ever contact her again. This made us a little suspicious but aside from the seat, there didn't seem to be anything wrong with the car so we gave her the money and I took ownership of my first and to this day only European car.

Things were great for the first two weeks or so. We took the car on all our adventures, including trips to the beach. Trouble started when the passenger side door lock mechanism failed. You could lock the door but could not unlock it using the key. You had to manually unlock it from the inside. No problem, I still had one working door lock. Two days later I ate my words. Outside the grocery store, I filled my trunk with groceries and returned the shopping cart. I unlocked the driver's door with my key like always and pulled on the door handle which promptly came off in my hands.

The passenger side door was locked so I was effectively locked out of the car.

I had no choice but to empty the groceries from the trunk onto the ground, crawl into the trunk and force the rear seat down in order to gain access to the interior. All this while my fellow shoppers looked on with amusement. It's a wonder that no one called the police! Until the broken door handle was eventually fixed, I had to open the door from the passenger's side and I could never lock the car again. Driving home from the grocery store, the end of the turn signal stalk broke and was hanging by a wire…I ended up taping it back on.

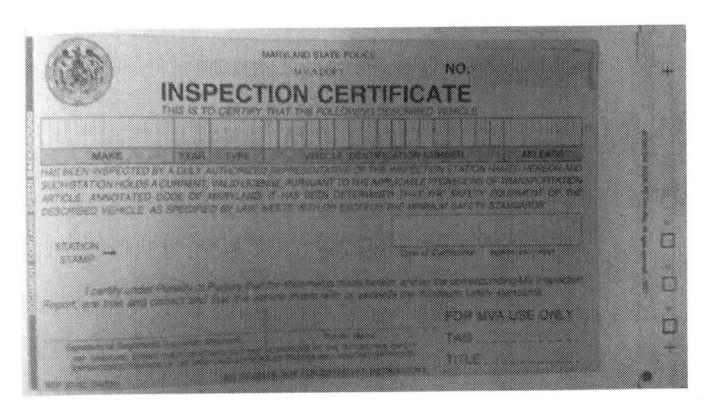

And the fun continued…. the car left me stranded twice in two weeks, once in a rain storm, the other in the dead of night on the side of the road due to electrical gremlins. By this time the Inspection deadline had passed. I knew it was not going to pass inspection but I had to get to work so I drove it anyway until the Maryland State Police also noticed that my inspection date was up…they said inspect it or else! I went to my bosses and told them the problem. They said to leave the car with them for the weekend. When I got the car back on Monday, it had a genuine, legal inspection certificate. I didn't ask.

For the next month or so, the car was OK besides the fact that I couldn't lock the doors (my bosses fixed the outside door handle that came off but the door lock was now broken). At this point the headliner began to disintegrate so whenever you exited the car you had what seemed like stardust flakes in your hair that you had to brush off. After this, the automatic transmission began to misbehave. In order to get sufficient power from the engine, you had to shift manually from 1 to 2 to 3.

By the way, the engine was actually very good. When it shifted properly, it was smooth and powerful and the car handled very well: it was the first car I had driven that could get me to triple digit speeds without feeling like I was at the edge of control. In addition, the AC blew ice cold all the time. Anyway, I did not mind the transmission so much...I just pretended I had a stick shift!

The car then began leaking coolant from the recovery bottle. At this point I had neither the money to get a new one from Saab nor have it installed so I went to a junkyard and found one from there and did my first ever DIY auto repair job...still proud of that to this day. The ultimate disaster struck maybe a month later when it refused to start. In the glove box, I found an old receipt from the dealer in the town where I bought the car. I called them to seek their advice. They knew the car immediately!

They said that the car was a total lemon and they had told the previous owner that it was no longer worth their while to work on it and it was good for parts only...they were appalled and distressed that the car was still on the road! They urged me to junk it immediately! Over the phone, they diagnosed the problem to be the starter; banging on it hard enough would make the car start. After they helped me with that, as with the previous owner they told me never to contact them again because there was nothing more they could do and did not want to feel responsible for what would happen if I continued to operate the car. Great!

The banging on the starter trick worked for a while but inevitably, the time came when it no longer started no matter how hard I banged on it. I checked with a local repair shop and it was $600 installed with a used starter! I was utterly dejected since I did not have the funds. My girlfriend and I shared her parents' reliable Mazda for a while until the need for two cars forced me to reluctantly make an SOS to Mom and Dad.

After the starter was fixed the car was actually pretty reliable and I took it on a few relatively long trips. However, I didn't quite trust it after all it put us through and I was always waiting for the other shoe to drop. At this time, my girlfriend was ready to buy her first brand new car, and we had gotten engaged a few months earlier so we used the Saab as her trade in.

One good thing that came out of this fiasco is that Mom and I bonded over it. She was encouraging and willing to listen to my Saab stories that I emailed her regularly to talk about what was happening with the Saab. She still has those e-mails to this day. In a sense, she was my first COAL reader.

At the time, because of my youth and extremely limited budget, I categorized this episode as my worst automotive decision ever. In retrospect, it really wasn't that bad. The car had nearly 200,000 miles on it – not bad for an 80's car – plus the entire experience cost me at most 1,500 bucks including the price of the car. Nearly ten years later, I would spend eight times that with nothing to show for it in what amounts to the worst auto decision I ever made. But that's a story for later on in this series.

My next COAL marks my return to my more traditional automotive choices.

1988 Dodge Aries America: "O K Car"

In my previous COAL, my experiment with a European car did not go well. In fact, by this time, I had gone through four cars in two and a half years! I needed some stability and some reliability. As usual, I didn't have much money but needed a car for work. My Dad's co-worker's husband owned a small used car business so Dad made a phone call and arranged a meeting. For $1,200, Dad's friend hooked me up with as he put it, "a vehicle that will not last you a lifetime but is solid and will give you a few years of service." I wasn't so sure about that but I had to be at work on Monday so I became the owner of a 1988 Dodge Aries America that looked just like the above picture...with 153,000 miles? Uh-oh! However, the salesman said..."don't worry about it...it's fine!" Surprisingly, he turned out to be right!

What exactly is an Aries America? From the brief research that I did, I learned that the America package was also applied to the Omni/Horizon and was essentially a value package that included equipment that was originally optional at reduced cost. For its final year in 1989, only the America version was offered. My car's interior looked identical to the picture above. Notice the wood trim and integrated cup holder. Another thing I noticed was the console mounted shifter. Prior to owning this car, I thought all K cars only came with column mounted shifters and bench seats. The bucket seats in my Aries America were actually quite comfortable.

It also came with this pivoting map light that folded neatly and unobtrusively into the passenger side sun visor that I found very useful. Although it kinda reminded me of the examination light in the dentist's office. I was actually quite impressed with the level of equipment and comfort that the car offered. I know, I know...I'm gushing about a K Car! To top it off, everything worked, including the air conditioning! Under the dash was a push in kill switch that disabled the starter which required a special key to disengage. The installation did not look at all aftermarket but very professional and almost factory. I'm still curious as to how it got there. It seemed like overkill for a Dodge Aries. Albeit the most well equipped Dodge Aries I'd ever experienced.

The powertrain consisted of the venerable 2.2 Liter four cylinder good for 99 horsepower and 121 lb./ft. of torque and console mounted automatic with lockup torque converter. While not a hot rod, it did have adequate power on the highway and accelerated smoothly and did not feel at all underpowered. In the handling department, I noticed that it did not feel loose or wallowy, even at higher speeds. I also remember that it got better gas mileage than my previous cars. This was helpful because my job at the time involved a lot of driving around to different sites.

The car seemed too good to be true, especially for an eleven year old K Car with 153,000 miles. A trip to the mechanic a few months later revealed the reason. It would seem that the salesman really did do my Dad a favor when he sold me the car. Apparently, the engine and transmission were not original but were newer units recently swapped in. The drivetrain had far less than the 153,000 miles on the body. In addition, the entire front end had been recently rebuilt with heavy duty parts explaining the unusually tight handling. Moreover, the entire undercarriage and frame had been reinforced.

1982 Plymouth Reliant squad (Grant Williams; at allpar.com)

I would like very much to know what this car was originally intended for. I know that there was a police package available for the early cars, but I did not think it was still available in '88. I have since learned that the local Fire Department where I bought the car used K cars as well as the State Government. I wonder if this was one of those vehicles.

This car turned out to be a great daily driver and long distance cruiser. It was economical, roomy and comfortable (I can't believe I'm talking about a K Car). Ownership turned out to be a nice respite to the automotive troubles I had suffered of late. I do recall one repair when the Check Engine Light illuminated followed by a loss of power. It turned out to be a faulty injector. The repair was not cheap but it was really the only one I had to do on the car. It did not bother me because unlike my previous cars, the repair solved it and it did not have chronic systemic issues that led to my being stranded or unsafe. In fact, in a reversal of roles, the K car and I rescued a few people who were stranded or were having automotive issues. It felt good to have something reliable for a change.

The car served me and my fiance well. We took it on many trips, especially our wedding planning trips. It even helped us move when we consolidated our households a few months before the wedding. It also served us well through a brief period of unemployment, needing nothing and taking me on my job interviews. I eventually landed another job which paid substantially more than my last one. For me, this meant an automotive upgrade was in order. I ended up selling it to an older gentleman who was going through tough times. Having recently gone through a similar situation, I was filled with empathy and let him have the car for $400. I hope the car was as good to him as it was to me. My next COAL was very much influenced by the good experience I had with this O K Car.

Act 1: 1992 Plymouth Acclaim

1992 Plymouth Acclaim & 1991 Chrysler New Yorker – "Pentastar Partners Redux"

I had just gotten a new job with a good raise (relatively speaking) and was ready for a newer car. I was very happy with my last COAL and was looking for something similar; namely, a reliable no frills conveyance. Since Dad found me my last vehicle, I asked him if he might be able to locate another "good one" for me again. Sure enough, he delivered in the form of a 42,000 mile one owner 1992 Plymouth Acclaim.

The AA bodies, the Chrysler LeBaron, Dodge Spirit and Plymouth Acclaim were evolved replacements of the K Cars. Engines ranged from the basic 100 hp 2.5 liter four which my car had, to the legendary 224 HP DOHC engine found in the Spirit RT

The previous owner of my Acclaim was an Executive of a large corporation who used the car as a daily driver/beater to commute to his office 10 miles away. In his garage, he had much nicer "high end" automobiles which he used for pleasure. The Acclaim was garage kept, well maintained, and immaculate. It was the nicest beater I had ever seen.

However, aside from automatic, cruise, and air, it was a stripper. It did not even have a radio!

The interior, while basic, was actually very nice. The seats were very comfortable for long trips. I installed a nice stereo and the car served me well as a daily driver. The internet picture above does not show it clearly, but in the actual car, there was a gap between the front bucket seats. I'm guessing a console was optional and not ordered. My wife thought it was great because her purse fit perfectly in that spot.

I found the instrument panel attractive as well. Straightforward and clear with cruise control switches on the steering wheel. I used the cruise a lot on our numerous

Maryland to New Jersey trips. I also liked the shelf above the climate control. It was perfect for storing parking and New Jersey Turnpike toll cards in the days before EZ Pass.

From a styling perspective, the front end bore a slight passing resemblance to a Mercedes Benz (or a [Plymouth Reliant](#)). I owned the car during the Chrysler merger with Daimler so my friends and family would tease me and say I owned a Mercedes!

1992 Acclaim (Plymouth photo at allpar.com)

From the beginning it was obvious that it was not a sports sedan. This is the only car that I have been pulled over in for going too slow! However, I must say that I found it to be smooth riding, competent, and quite comfortable.

My best memory of the car is Christmas night in 1999. We had just gotten the car and were driving my wife's grandmother back to her home in Perry Hall, Maryland. I remember her sitting in the back seat remarking…"Fred, this is a nice car…what kind of car is this? I like this car!" When we got back to her house, she lit up her Christmas decorations, and we had a nice Christmas celebration just the three of us. That night, I felt that she became my Grandmother too.

Aside from minor driver's door damage from a hit and run while the car was parked which I never did fix, the car needed nothing. Despite "extended" oil change intervals, it stayed true, never once stranding me or needing a single repair.

Prior to getting this car, my vehicles figured very prominently in my memories. I realize now that this was in part because the "eccentric" qualities of my previous cars ensured that any trip in them was far from uneventful. This car was the opposite, despite the fact that huge life milestones like getting married, buying a house, and moving back to New Jersey occurred during my ownership of this car. Aside from the Christmas memory I wrote about above, it does not figure prominently in my remembrances of those days. Maybe it's because it worked as it should and nothing ever went wrong with it.

In the end, that's why I got rid of it. It was pretty boring albeit very reliable, one of the most reliable cars I have ever owned. One day, on my way home from work, I saw a car from my past, a car that I always wanted. Impulsively that afternoon, the Acclaim was replaced by a <u>future COAL which you will read about in two weeks.</u>

Act 2: 1991 Chrysler New Yorker

My past few cars had been fairly utilitarian vehicles and I was having some serious Brougham withdrawal. Dad and his extra cars came to the rescue again.

In a **previous COAL**, I talked about my Dad's policy of keeping extra cars around "in case someone needs them," he would say. This time he had just the thing to cure my Brougham longings...a 1991 Chrysler New Yorker with 114,000 "little old lady" miles. Like my **previous K car based "luxury sedans,"** the C Body New Yorkers were also derived from the **K Car.** At the time, I was looking for something unique and traditionally comfortable. This vehicle delivered the goods.

On the inside, it had the fake wood and front bench seat that was standard fare on the American land yachts that I knew and loved.

On the outside, it had the oh so familiar upright grill with hood ornament, hidden headlights, and landau roof. While it did have strange proportions, it had all the prerequisite trimmings.

I had first encountered this generation of New Yorker when I stayed over a friend's house for Spring Break a few years back. His Dad had a brand new one. It had the Bill Blass look as described here. I remember going out to dinner in it. Comfortable blue leather seats, smooth ride, and the soulful sound of Kenny G playing from its Chrysler Infinity sound system.

When my Dad gave us use of his New Yorker, we became a three car family with my wife's car (next week's COAL), my Plymouth Acclaim, mentioned above, and the New Yorker. We now had more cars than people.

Introducing the all new Chrysler New Yorker.
It gives you the one thing
you always wanted in a luxury car.
Everything.

Our New Yorker was brown with wire wheels. The exterior was flawless and the car was obviously garage kept.

The interior was red cloth and very comfortable. Yes, it did have the weird proportions, and the mini limo look but I found it roomy, especially the trunk. Maybe it was because it was just my wife and I; so there was plenty of room for the two of us. It did make for a pretty good daily driver.

Mechanically speaking, while reliable, the car seemed tired. There was a strange creaking and squeaking coming from the front end. Also, the 3.3 liter V6 engine ran OK but according to the oil pressure gauge, read a bit on the low side when the car warmed up. Enough to make me a little nervous anyway.

I eventually traded it and my Plymouth Acclaim for a <u>COAL you will be reading about in two weeks</u>.

This post is so titled because it is so deja vu with <u>my COAL from a few weeks back</u>. Both involved my Dad and his extra cars. It also made me rethink what I thought was my Dad's affinity for GM cars. In writing this series, it made me realize that he had quite a few memorable Mopar vehicles in his collection as well.

1998 Chevrolet Cavalier – "The Return of J Love"

(Except for the Cavalier in wedding regalia, the pictures in this post were borrowed from Google image search)

This COAL is dedicated to my LOAL (Love of a Lifetime), my wife, Tiffany

As stated in my <u>second COAL</u>, when I first started driving, I had a thing for <u>J cars</u>. However, after my third experience, I moved on to other vehicles. I did have some seat time in other J cars owned by family and friends, and while I could see the minor improvements over my early examples, I did not think they were that much of an improvement…been there, done that. That is, until 1995.

1995 was the year that the Cavalier and its surviving sister car, the Sunbird (now renamed Sunfire) received a major makeover. I had the opportunity to have a close look when a friend of mine got one. Compared to my 84 and 85 models, the new Cavalier was the epitome of refinement. Gone was the <u>Cadillac Cimarron</u> styling, which was replaced by the round look shared by the refreshed <u>B bodies</u> which were my dream cars at the time. In addition, the tail lights had hints of the <u>'95 Camaro</u> as well.

Yes...it was also sold in Japan as a Toyota....enough said. More info <u>here</u> if anyone is interested.

The interiors were modern and contemporary looking; similar to the Camaro as well. There was a real center console, and like the '95 Caprice, rotary switches for the climate control replacing the cheap slider controls of cars past. The seats felt more substantial and less "jump seat like" than my previous Cavaliers. In addition, it had the same safety systems that contemporary high end cars of the day had namely, daytime running lights, dual air bags and anti lock brakes. This was enough to rekindle my love for J cars.

Sure enough, when it came time for my fiance (now my wife) to get a new car, I convinced her to give the Cavalier a try. She purchased her Cavalier shortly before our wedding. It was a nice metallic blue color, which she loved. Unfortunately, she owned the car for about three months when it sacrificed its life to save hers when an Explorer lost control on the Baltimore Washington Parkway and skidded into her. The Explorer actually flipped over onto its roof. Very scary! Miraculously, no one was injured, but her beautiful blue Cavalier was totaled!

As soon as the insurance check came, we promptly looked for another; grateful for the safety features that helped keep her from serious harm. The replacement was identical to the original car except for its metallic green color. It was a pretty basic model besides a cassette player, automatic transmission, air conditioning, and a rear window defroster. In fact, this was our last car with manual crank windows and manual door locks. However, to us, it was state of the art. It was our first car with dual air bags and anti lock brakes.

It had a three speed automatic transmission and the base engine, a 2.2 liter 4 cylinder with 115 horsepower.

Although this was my wife's primary vehicle, I got to drive it on many occasions. Compared to my previous J cars, the car did not feel underpowered. While there were times that it became obvious that it did not have unlimited power, I felt that I could make full use of the power it did have, unlike my <u>previous J cars</u> which felt and sounded like the warp core would explode like on Captain Kirk's *Enterprise* whenever he ordered Scotty to floor it. I also found that it handled better than my old Cavaliers. Gas mileage was OK if not great.

One thing I will never forget is this is the car that we started our married life with. Here you see our wedding guests "decorating" the car for the occasion.

Here's a picture of the car after they were done with it. After the wedding reception, we drove it to our honeymoon to begin our life together in Holy Matrimony.

Shortly after our wedding, we decided to move to back to my home state of New Jersey from Maryland. Since we were saving our money for a down payment on a house, we used both my Plymouth Acclaim and the Cavalier as moving vans. Cramming them with our stuff and making multiple trips back and fourth. One time we over filled the Cavalier's trunk and broke off a plastic connector that prevented the trunk from being opened except by folding down the seat, crawling into the trunk, and triggering the emergency release. What a pain! We repaired it but were annoyed at the cheap plastic that caused such an inconvenient failure. The other thing we discovered was that the seats became very uncomfortable and painful on long trips.

Other than that, the only things we replaced were a battery and tires and a small oil leak which we repaired. It was also with this car that I learned about GM's "Check Gages (as opposed to Check Gauges)" light which illuminated when fuel ran low or something else was amiss like the car was overheating. Thankfully, the light only came on for us because we were low on gas and not for anything more serious. I still wondered why GM spelled "gages" like this. A quick search of Dictionary.com revealed this:

"The spelling variants gauge and gage have existed since the first recorded uses in Middle English, though inAmerican English gage is found exclusively in technical uses."

This car, along with my last COAL , helped us begin our married life. We took this car everywhere...it was our default car whenever we went anywhere as a couple.

We moved into the first house we owned with this car. It took us to our job interviews in New Jersey and when the time came, to the many doctor's appointments when we decided it was time to start a family. We ended up keeping the car for five years and it was the best J car that I have ever owned. In 2004, we had our first child and we needed something bigger to accommodate car seat, stroller, and other paraphernalia. So eventually, my wife began to use **next week's COAL as the baby hauler. Hint: Another larger Chevy from my past.**

1991 Chevrolet Caprice – "Living Up to a Legend"

This COAL is dedicated to my oldest son Samuel, who first came home in this car.

In our house, **my long departed 78 Caprice** was an object of reverence. That car personified good times, road trips, friendships and coming of age. Anytime I brought up my past, the car was inevitably included in my stories. It was a legend that occupied a place of honor in the Lore of Fred. In my eyes, the Caprice could do no wrong. I never regretted giving it up because it was in the spirit of friendship that I let it go, but in my heart I knew I wanted to have another Caprice someday.

Introduced in 1990 as early '91s, GM radically restyled its surviving full-size, rear-wheel drive B bodies. In addition to the new rounded look, the cars also gained anti-lock brakes and a driver's side airbag. The new look was very polarizing. People either loved them or hated them. As for me, I remember the day an auto transporter delivered them to Multi Chevrolet in Union, NJ. I had no idea which Chevy it was..... a Lumina, maybe? I had to go find out. When I learned it was a Caprice...I got goosebumps! I loved the new look! The Caprice name had always meant something to me, and I was very pleased that the car had been modernized to go with the times. Yes, it had an airbag and ABS, but still had V8 power and rear-wheel drive! It even had a cameo in my favorite movie at the time,*Days of Thunder*. From that day on, I wanted one!

Not the actual car or car dealer

One day, while driving home from work in my <u>Plymouth Acclaim</u>, I passed a used car lot where I saw it. The gray 1991 Chevrolet Caprice with 63,000 miles filled my heart with desire. To me it represented the <u>Caprice of my youth</u> as well as the Caprice body style I always wanted. I wanted it at all costs! Because I had no money (as usual), I traded in two cars, m<u>y '92 Acclaim, and '91 New Yorker,</u> for the Caprice. It was not an even trade, as more cash was required by the seller for it to be mine. I gladly ponied up (how much, I am embarrassed to say). I knew I paid more than it was worth, but I didn't care at this point. I even let them talk me into paying extra for the warranty.

Driving home in the car of my dreams, I was on cloud nine! I absolutely loved it...it was all I expected and more. I had to swing by Mom and Dad's to show off my prize!

Thank God they were not home since what happened next would have been really embarassing. As we were leaving their house, the Check Engine light came on. Then it began to lose power and finally stall. It restarted but could not be kept running at idle. I had to either keep going or put it in neutral and give it some gas. We headed right back to the used car lot only to find that it had closed for the day. We headed over the next day, and I could not have been happier that I allowed them to talk me into getting the warranty—as it turned out, the car needed a new Electronic Control Module (ECM), which was nowhere near cheap. It was replaced at no cost to me, and the car was finally in good running condition.

For 1991, the restyled B bodies came standard with the 5.0-liter 305 V8 with TBI Injection, otherwise known as the LO3. This engine was rated at 170 HP with 255 lb-ft of torque. Taxi (9C6) and police (9C1) package vehicles had several options: Most had the 5.7-liter 350 V8, also with TBI injection, known as the LO5 and rated at 180 HP with 290 lb-ft of torque. Rarer still (and I'm not even sure of its authenticity) was a 4.3-liter 140

HP V6 (not to be confused with the 4.3 liter L99 V8 from 94-96) offered for fleet use only in 1992-1993. I read about only one documented vehicle with this engine many years ago, but I have not seen any pictures or read about any others that still exist. For 1992-1993 the LO5 V8 became optional on sedans and standard on wagons. There was also the LTZ version, which was essentially a police package car but with all the luxury trimmings, and the precursor to the 94-96 Impala SS. The 94-96 vehicles came with two new and more powerful engine options based on the Corvette LT 1 engine, which will be discussed in a future COAL.

You can always tell a '91 model by its black B- and C-pillars and black door handle trim. Later models wore them in body color. My car was a Caprice, as opposed to the better equipped Caprice Classic pictured above. The base Caprice was equivalent to Biscaynes of the past, but this one's previous owner had opted for power windows and locks, and the car was air conditioned.

The interior was very 1962. Horizontal speedometer, idiot lights (although LTZ models had a full set of gauges) and a front bench seat. I must say, the seating was very comfortable and wonderful for long trips. After a long day at work, it was wonderful to plop down into that seat at the end of the day. The air conditioning, on the other hand, was pretty weak despite the fact that it had recently been filled and sealed with new refrigirant. It was fine in the late spring or early summer, but when the temperature rose above 90, it was embarrassing and ineffective even when set to maximum.

Just like on **my first Caprice**, the trunk was pretty enormous. Needless to say, interior space was generous as well. I regularly carried six people in the car without feeling terribly cramped.

I did very much appreciate the torque on the 305 V8. Off-the-line pickup was good, occasionally even chirping the tires...not that I minded, of course. It was fun blowing away Neons and such at traffic lights. Its main problem was that it ran out of breath quickly. I remember following my parents in their 2004 Camry on the highway. Accelerating on the on ramp was fun and I was on their bumper until about 80 MPH or so. After that, I could still keep up with them but I noticed the engine working hard to do so.

It made a great daily driver. It was comfortable, reliable, and relatively low maintenance. Here it is pictured next to last week's COAL.

In 2004, our first child, Samuel, was born. We took him home in the Caprice. It soon became obvious that this was the perfect car for him. The large trunk could easily hold his stroller, his play pen, and whatever else he could possibly need. Its spacious interior could accommodate the cumbersome rear-facing child seat that newborns require AND carry additional passengers in comfort. Most importantly, its sheer heaviness and tank-like construction made us feel safe transporting our most precious cargo.

The writing was on the wall. My wife would be taking over the Caprice since she was home with Sam. Here she is, posing with her new daily driver. As for me, I had not yet gotten B-bodies out of my system, so I sold the Cavalier in order to get my next daily driver, the subject of next week's COAL.

1991 Chevrolet Caprice 9C1 – "Corvette Power"

After my experience with last week's COAL, I was hooked. Except this time, I was searching for the ultimate Caprice. Starting in 1994, Caprices had two engine choices, both derived from the LT1 engine that powered the C4 Corvette from 1992-1996. That's right…the Corvette. The two engines were the 4.3-liter L99 version, with 200 HP for fuel economy, found in standard Caprices; and the 5.7-liter LT1, with 260 HP for performance, found in station wagons and optional on sedans and the 9C1 police-package cars. Used Caprices were cheap back then, especially retired 9C1 police-package Caprices. So for less than $2,500, one could obtain a decent example with Corvette power. In my opinion this was the best kept secret of American car enthusiasts. Needless to say, my requirements for the "ultimate Caprice" included an LT1-powered example with the 9C1 package (which included items such as four-wheel disc anti lock brakes, limited slip differential, motor and transmission oil coolers, heavy duty alternator, frame, and suspension, as well as a calibrated speedometer). I also preferred a '95 model, since that was the year they got the large foldaway heated side mirrors vs. the smaller, "bullet style" units.

I found one for sale online. It was located about 3 miles from me, had 105,000 miles on the odometer and was priced at $2,000. I took it home for $1,800 cash. I was extremely pleased with my purchase, a white ex-Hanover, NJ police cruiser.

Thankfully, there were no police stickers that had to be removed. There were holes in the roof and trunk that had been plugged, as well as holes in the dashboard. It still had the extremely bright **ticket writing light** behind the rearview mirror, as well as the driver's side spotlight. I found both extremely helpful at night. The ticket writing light was helpful when reading or filing out paperwork at night and the spotlight for illuminating our door when we came home late at night. There was also a "stealth button" on the dash that killed all illumination inside the car including the dash lighting. It is my understanding that this feature was used on stakeouts to prevent the dash lighting from reflecting on the driver's face and betraying the fact that someone was in the vehicle watching the bad guys.

The car had a blue interior with cloth-covered front buckets (which had anti-stab metal built into the seatbacks to protect the driver and front passenger), a vinyl rear bench seat and rubber floor for easy cleaning. The AC and all power accessories worked. Unlike my <u>civilian '91 Caprice</u>, the AC in this car was quite effective. Since the car was an in-town unit, it did not have cruise control. The austere interior appointments worked to our advantage the day after Thanksgiving, when my son was about six months old. We were coming back to Jersey from Maryland and, sure enough, there was a car fire and accident on the Delaware Memorial Bridge and a few accidents on I-95. This turned our usual four-hour trip into a nine-hour odyssey stuck in gridlocked traffic with no place to pull over. Thankfully, the heavy duty cooling system allowed for endless idling without fear of overheating. In addition, we had to do about four diaper changes (filled with the heavy stuff) and multiple Gerber feedings in the car while stuck in traffic. The vinyl rear seat and rubber floor made clean up simple after we finally got home. There was no stained upholstery to worry about.

The previous owner had tried to make an Impala SS clone out of it. He ordered and installed the leaping deer symbols on the side as well as an Impala SS grille. I prefer the stock look myself (especially since the Impala SS was never offered in white) and quickly replaced the grille with a stock '95 Caprice grille. I did not remove the leaping deer emblems for fear of damaging the paint.

Actually, I prefer the 9C1 to the Impala SS because it has the same engine, but also has a higher ground clearance and indestructible green "lifetime" hoses in the engine compartment. I saw the 9C1 as a "ruggedized" Impala SS for daily use and abuse.

For 1993, Chevrolet opened up the rear wheel wells and revised the tail lights on the sedans in an attempt to improve the "bloated whale" look of the 91-92 cars. Model Year 1994 brought revised interiors with a passenger-side airbag, climate controls with rotary switches and a digital dash with Corvette styling cues.

As you can see from this pic, the previous owner, Matt, installed a custom air intake and air cleaner system which allowed the engine to breathe better–not that it needed it. The LT1 delivered as promised. The car was fast. Snap-your-neck fast. It started with an aggressive roar, and acceleration was simply amazing...one uninterrupted burst of power. It did not stop accelerating strongly...it was I who ended up letting off the gas for fear of going too fast. It lived for triple digit speeds. It was easily the fastest, best handling car that I have ever owned.

Despite the lack of cruise control, it was great on long trips. It was very roomy, and the engine and suspension made driving very entertaining. I remember once on a whim, we decided to drive from Northern NJ to Annapolis MD for dinner. It was a very easy, very fun, very relaxing sunset trip. On the way down I-95, we encountered a pack of at least 20 bikers on Harley Davidsons. They formed a cordon around the Caprice and "escorted" us south at high speed, giving us thumbs up all the way.

I was so proud of the car that I didn't want just anyone servicing it. After doing some research, I found a shop about ten minutes from where I lived that specialized in LT1 cars. To try them out I made an appointment for an oil change late in the day.

Photo from Google Image Search

The shop was quite impressive. It looked like the Hot Wheels service station playset I had as a kid. There were about four Corvettes there and two Buick Grand Nationals in the service bay.

The owner was very nice. He hoisted my car on the lift as his assistant drained the oil. He complimented my decision to buy the car saying that the Caprice/LT1 package was "absolutely bulletproof." He gave the car a quick inspection and everything checked out.

He did want to give the steering a closer look, but he said that could wait until next time. All that was left to to do was reset the "Change Oil" light on the dashboard. This was done by pumping the gas twice within four seconds with the ignition in the "run" position. The first few tries were unsuccessful and he was getting impatient so he jammed his steel-toed boots down as hard as he could several times until the light finally went off.

I thanked him for taking me so close to closing time and drove off. I was about a block away when all of a sudden, the gas pedal became unresponsive and the car could only creep forward very slowly. The 4L60E transmission was the Achilles heel of this platform so I was sure that this was the issue here. I felt sick knowing that there was no way I could afford a new transmission. I turned around and crept slowly back to the shop. Sure enough, it was closed and locked up tight. I banged hard on the door anyway and the assistant who helped change the oil appeared. Upon investigating the problem, it turned out that the accelerator cable had come loose and was no longer connected to the throttle. Five minutes later, I was back in business. I never did return to that shop. Everything was great after that. I took the car everywhere and it was a reliable daily driver. I did notice an occasional creaking coming from the front end, but the car seemed to drive fine otherwise.

Photo from Google Image Search

One day as I was turning into my parking space at work, I heard a loud bang and the car was tilted at the left front. I slowly completed my turn into the space with loud grinding and scraping. At first I thought I got a flat tire but upon further inspection, I noticed the tire tilted at an odd angle. It was not a flat. The lower control arm, tie rod, and shock absorber had failed, causing the front wheel to become partially detached from the car! Great!

I had it repaired, but somehow it did not seem to be the same after that. I did not have as much fun driving it and began to look for a replacement. Sure enough, a few weeks later, I found something that would fulfill my car buying requirements for the next five years.

1993 Buick Roadmaster – "The Not So Daily Driver"

(All the pictures in this post are from Google Image Search)

This post is in memory of Helen Augsburger (1916-2005), my Grandmother-in-Law, who was mentioned in a previous COAL.

I had gotten a new job in Jersey City, NJ, just outside Manhattan and did not want to subject my 9C1 to the abuses of daily city driving. Consequently, I began to search for a beater/city daily driver. While driving around, I encountered a '93 Saturn with a for sale sign reading $300. I pulled over, called the number and waited for the seller to show up.

It was a gold sedan with about 70,000 miles. It drove well and it did not seem to have any issues. He said that he was selling the car for his daughter. It seemed like the perfect city car. I asked him why he was selling so cheap, and he said he just wanted it gone as soon as possible. I told him I wanted the car. He said, "OK, give me the money." I told him that I had just seen the car and would need to go to an ATM but would be back in 20 minutes. He told me that would not be acceptable, that he needed it gone now. I told him if he waited 20 minutes, I'd pay him $400. He said he wasn't sure, but I told him I'd be back in 20 minutes tops with the money. I came back maybe 15 minutes later to find the car gone. I tried calling him; no answer. I waited around and saw him coming down the street. He took one look at me and took off running in the other direction. To this day, I don't know what that was about. Now that I think of it, I was in my 9C1 when I came to see him. Maybe he did not really own the car and he thought I was law enforcement? Oh well, I guess I'll never know.

A few weeks later, I found a local car for sale that I thought would work. It was a white 1992 Buick Roadmaster station wagon with "woody" flanks and a tan leather interior. It had the 180 hp LO5 350 V8 and the towing package, which included oil and transmission coolers, heavy duty suspension and limited slip differential. The car had 136,000 miles on the odo and I took it home for about $1,400. The car had some trim pieces missing, including the hood ornament, the driver's seat was torn and the glove box was broken, but otherwise it was pretty solid. There was one other thing: The anti-lock feature of the brakes was inoperative and the warning light was on. The brakes were fine, otherwise. This is where I used a skill I learned from my J car days, using black electrical tape to cover up annoying warning lights. The plan was to use the Roadmaster as a beater/daily driver and have the 9C1 as a weekend car.

When I got the car home, I realized it was a lot nicer than I'd given it credit for. The Roadmaster wagons were the premier luxury wagons of their time, probably equivalent to today's Cadillac Escalade. Mine was the first car that I'd owned that had genuine leather seats. Prior to owning this car, I thought leather seats were just like vinyl seats; I learned the error of my ways quickly. The soft feel, even the smell of the leather, convinced me that leather seats and vinyl seats were not the same.

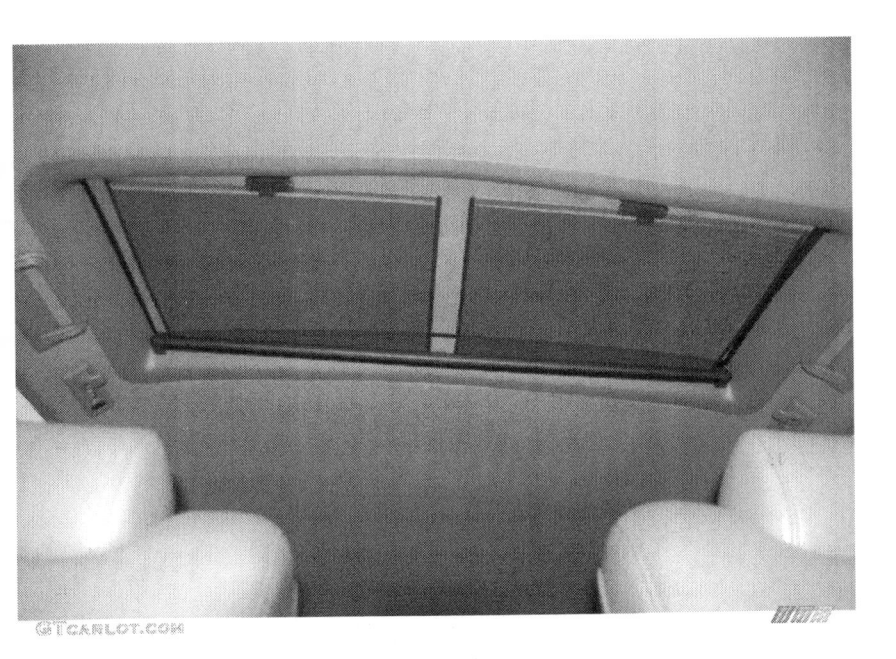

The Buick Roadmasters and Oldsmobile Custom Cruisers of this generation also had a Vista Roof over the second-row seats. I thought it was a nice touch that really brightened up the interior. It was also loaded with such luxury features as electronic climate control, power seats, twilight sentinel, power everything and auto-dimming rear view mirror. This car was much more comfortable and well equipped than anything I'd ever owned before.

The Corvette-derived LT1 engine became standard in the 1994-96 Roadmasters. In addition, the interiors were redesigned with, among other things, a new dashboard. I actually prefer the earlier dashes as depicted above, since they included a full set of gauges. Also, the TBI engines in the 1991-93 cars were less complex and easier to work on than those in the LT1 cars. In addition, they had the far less troublesome 700R transmission, as opposed to the more troublesome 4L60E of the LT1 cars.

For me, the most important discovery was the HUGE cargo area. I thought my Caprice sedan trunks were large, but this was something else entirely. I was able to easily transport recliners, wheelbarrows, lawn mowers, Christmas trees, baby items, you name it. It was like having a covered pickup truck. A few weeks ago, I was reading Robert Kim's COAL about his Custom Cruiser wagon and I couldn't agree more about the cargo capacity and utility of these vehicles.

As I mentioned above, the supple leather seats and the power amenities ensured that any ride in the Roadmaster was comfortable and luxurious. While I had originally purchased this car to keep the 9C1 from doing the daily city commute, I began to really appreciate the Roadmaster more than the Caprice. As a result, the opposite happened: The Roadmaster stayed in the garage and the 9C1 became the daily driver, a role that it was very well suited to.

A few weeks ago, I mentioned that I had grown close to my wife's grandmother. Sadly, she passed away in the summer of 2005. We took the Roadmaster to Maryland for the funeral and to be with family. It was during those days that I discovered yet another positive attribute of the car, the foldaway rear-facing third seat. Helen's death brought family together, and it was a reunion of sorts for my wife, her three siblings and their spouses. Lunches and get togethers were arranged since we were all together, and the increased seating capacity of the car allowed us to all travel to lunch in one vehicle. It was actually pretty impressive. More importantly, it allowed us all to spend some very good times together. I think my Grandmother-in-Law would have approved. I can still hear her voice when she said about <u>another vehicle of mine</u> "this is a nice car Fred....what kind of car is this?"

As I mentioned at the end of my last <u>COAL</u>, my 9C1 had fallen out of favor with me, so I replaced it with <u>next week's COAL</u>. At about the same time, one of my good friends was down a car so I let him have the Roadmaster, as he needed it badly for work and family obligations. Soon he, too, appreciated its utility when he used it to haul a playground set (including a tree house) for his kids. He was not known to be gentle with cars, yet that car served him faithfully until its engine died at about 200,000 miles.

The Roadmaster left big shoes to fill and also set the standard for all my future cars over the next five years. They all had to be V8 powered, and they all had to have third-row seating and a large cargo capacity.

As you will see, my next seven COALs, in one way or another, met those requirements.

1998 Chevrolet Caprice – "Distinctive Aroma"

(The images for this post were taken from Google image search)

I was looking to replace my 9C1. I knew I wanted another B-body, and I was very impressed by the utility of my Roadmaster Estate wagon. Searching online, I found a brown 1988 Chevrolet Caprice Estate with fake wood siding and 44,000 one-owner miles. I was immediately intrigued because it reminded me so much of my first Caprice.

The car was at Wigder Chevrolet in East Hanover, New Jersey, where it had been purchased and serviced since new. Its original owner was getting on in years and needed something smaller, so she'd traded it in for a brand new Malibu Maxx. Aside from a small dent on the driver's side fender, the exterior was in nice shape. The paint was still shiny, and the fake wood looked fresh. It was obvious that this was a garage-kept car. Underneath, there was some rust, but nothing unusual for a nearly 20-year-old car in the Northeast.

The cloth interior was in excellent shape. It was not at all faded, the carpet was mint and there were no rips in the upholstery. The car was fully optioned out with power seats, windows, locks and antenna, plus a premium sound system. It also came equipped with three details I thought were available only on Buicks, Oldsmobiles, and Cadillacs: It had Twilight Sentinel, exterior cornering lamps, and a tiny spotlight that shined directly on the headlight switch so you could see it at night when you started the car. To be clear, the switch was not backlit; there literally was a tiny spotlight that highlighted the headlight switch when you started the car. I had never before seen such a classy-broughamy detail on a Chevy.

The other feature I really liked was the power-operated rear window. Unlike the Roadmaster, the rear window was not held up by failure-prone struts; it rolled neatly into the tailgate. I loved how you could roll the window up and down by using the door key, and that the window could also be controlled by a button on the dash.

While my Roadmaster was nice, it obviously was used; this car, on the other hand, appeared to be very lightly used. What's more, it met the criteria I'd set at the end of my last COAL, it was V8 powered, and it had a third row of seats in the event that we had to transport guests. So a deal was struck, and after I'd handed over the 9C1 plus 700 bucks, I was the new owner of this survivor and near classic.

The car was equipped with a four-speed automatic with overdrive, and powered by an Oldsmobile 307 V8 rated at 140 HP and with 255 lb./ft. of torque. This engine was put in new GM B-bodies until 1990 and was the last carbureted engine GM put into a car sold in the U.S. Ninety percent of everything I have read about this engine is not kind–in fact, it's often referred to as a "dog." Sources list its "theoretical" top speed at 103 mph, a 0-60 time of 13 seconds and a 19-second quarter mile– unimpressive for such a large engine. The relatively better performing Chevy 305 was offered as an option, but my car was not so equipped.

I experienced the problem driving it home: the car was S-L-O-W and seemed vastly under-powered, although I did appreciate how smooth and silent the engine was. Remember, I was coming from a 260 hp, LT1-equipped V8 car. I was on it pretty hard, but it did not seem like it was straining at all. It did not get loud or harsh or feel like it was going to explode. It was just S-L-O-W. On the highway, it was difficult to maintain 70 MPH. I was beginning to think that I'd made a big mistake.

I took it for an emissions inspection, which it failed. I was not surprised, since the engine was literally covered with emissions-related hoses and equipment! So, the plugs and air cleaner were changed, the carburetor was serviced (incidentally, this was the last carb-equipped vehicle I owned), and the EGR system was overhauled.

After its time in the shop, not only did it pass inspection but performance greatly improved. It did not accelerate like the 9C1, but it did accelerate like a proper V8 and no longer struggled to cruise past 70. In fact, on interstate trips I could cruise in the far left lane the entire time and cars actually moved over to let me by.

I have been told that the 307 had a lot of potential, but had been deliberately detuned for the sake of smoothness and longevity. I do know that despite its leisurely performance, this engine has a reputation for lasting upwards of 300,000 miles. While I was OK with its performance, fuel economy was another story, as I was getting between 16-18 mpg on a good day.

Its utility did not disappoint me. I regularly used its third-row seat as well as its impressive cargo-carrying ability. It was around this time that we sold our house and moved into an apartment while we searched for our new home. That meant a lot of our things had to go into storage until we found a house we were interested in buying. I discovered one of those <u>cargo bags that you secure to a roof rack on an SUV</u> which, along with the 87 cubic feet of space in the cargo area, really simplified our move. In fact, most of the move was done using this car and my buddy's <u>(and my former) Roadmaster wagon</u>. I am reminded again about <u>Robert Kim's experience with his Olds wagon.</u>

One other thing: B-body wagons have an almost 50-50 weight distribution, which made it awesome in snow. Indeed, that car handled deep snow better than many of my front-wheel drive vehicles. I was afraid that its carbureted engine would make cold starting difficult, but that was not the case—two pumps of the gas pedal prior to starting was all it took for reliable winter starts. I've also read that the "mild" gearing (for fuel economy), combined with the mild 307 engine, contributed to its surefootedness.

The car was my daily driver. Fuel economy aside, it was comfortable, practical and enjoyable to drive. There is, however, one unfortunate thing I've not mentioned so far: I was the only one who could stand to sit in its luxurious interior. Why? The cabin had a foul odor that was hard to describe. The odor could best be described as smelling biological–hair, sweat, vomit, feces, spit and urine. The smell was there when I bought the car, but I thought I could take care of it and it would eventually go away. Boy, was I wrong! We tried everything: baking soda, shampoo, air freshener, pouring perfume on the seats, even driving with all windows open (at 80 mph) for a week. Nothing worked. I remember picking up my mother in law from the train station one time. Within ten seconds, she remarked, "Oh my God, what is that smell?" The worst thing was that the smell would stick to your clothes, so pretty soon you were carrying the odor on your person, just like in the *Seinfeld* episode.

So I began a passive search once more. It did not take long before I encountered what was to me, at the time, the ultimate B-body....the Holy Grail (and I don't mean an Impala SS)...and the subject of next week's COAL.

1995 Caprice Wagon – "The Holy LT1 Grail"

From the past few COALs I had learned a few things: 1) I was in love with the B body design 2) I missed the LT1 performance of my 9C1 3) I liked the white non-descript color of my 9C1 4) the utility of the B body wagon was essential 5) I liked cushy brougham interiors 6) I liked the big fold away heated side view mirrors of the 95-96 B bodies.

I was passively searching for a replacement for my last COAL because nobody wanted to ride in it anymore and came upon the following:

1) 1995 Chevrolet Caprice wagon with big, fold-away heated side view mirrors

2) Cranberry red cloth interior with power windows, locks, seats and antenna

3) Bright white exterior with no fake wood (a huge bonus for me)

4) Station wagon with third-row seat

5) 5.7 liter LT1 V8 with 260 HP

6) Definitely a B-body

My car with a friend's New York City driven but only 30,000 original mile '87 (Che)'Vette

A point-for-point match...it couldn't get any better than that. It looked like a wagon version of my 9C1. It was not easy convincing my wife to support me in bringing home yet another B-body. Eventually, she grudgingly relented and I made the appointment to see the car, knowing full well there was no way I was leaving without it.

The car was at a small used car dealership in Belleville, not far from where I work. When I saw it, I was even more convinced that *I had to have it.* It was a one-owner car with about 120,000 miles on it. The car spent its winters in Florida which accounted for the non existent rust underneath. Moreover, the car had recently had its transmission rebuilt. I saw this as a good thing because these cars were equipped with the 4L60E transmission, about which I have heard many horror stories of early failure. I was glad that this car's trans had already been redone.

The cranberry red cloth upholstery was in good condition. One thing that I did not mention in my previous write-ups about these cars is that the window rollers were very common failure items on the 91-96 B bodies which resulted in windows coming off the track and not being able to close properly unless manually guided upward by hand. This wagon was afflicted with this problem, which rendered the left rear passenger window inoperative. The fix was apparently very easy but I did not have the proper tools to remove the door panel as required. In addition, the factory cassette player was not working. The radio worked fine but it would not accept cassettes. This was not really a problem, since most of my music was on CDs and I was slowly transitioning to MP3s. I had one of those transmitters that allowed me to play my portable music trough an unused radio frequency on the car stereo.

The **Corvette derived LT1** ran well and was recently serviced. I did find that the suspension was much softer than my **9C1** but this was to be expected since it did not have the police or towing package. By the way, Chevy did have a special service/police package for Caprice wagons, called the 1A2. Only 846 were made so they are relatively rare. Unfortunately, the few I have encountered were pretty well used up. Finally, like my **previous Roadmaster wagon**, the anti-lock feature of the brakes was no longer working. I wonder if this was a common failure item with these cars. I had another B-body wagon after this with this exact problem.

Despite these issues, I was sure that I would not be looking for another car again....I finally had my dream car. It was a very nice car that I maintained meticulously—at first (although I never did repair the misaligned window or ABS light). This was in part due to a fuel pump failure early in my ownership that was not cheap to repair and broke my budget in terms of repair/improvements to the car aside from the installation of XM satellite radio. I did make sure oil changes and such were done according to schedule.

I must say the Caprice wagon was a fine vehicle. It was competent, comfortable and fun. Like my last two wagons, it could haul an impressive amount of stuff. For example, our current dining set was delivered via the Caprice wagon. In one trip that car hauled the dining table, diner-style sectional bench, and three dining chairs. The other customers where I bought the furniture, many with full sized pickup trucks, watched in disbelief as the entire dining set fit in the wagon and on the roof rack. Later that same day, I used the Caprice to deliver an oversize antique sofa to my brother-in-law's home in Baltimore.

It was equally great at transporting people. There is a state park close to where we live that charges admission per car, regardless of the number of occupants. Whenever we had guests over and decided to spend a day at the park, we would take advantage of the Caprice's eight passenger seating and save on the admission fee. As with my Roadmaster wagon, my family and four guests could all go out to dinner in one car. I figured I basically had a Suburban that was lower to the ground with a more potent engine....sweet!

Handling was nowhere near as tight as my 9C1 but it handled pretty competently. The LT1 pulled strongly and was entertaining in a straight line. I remember one Sunday morning, I had to get to an early morning graduation. It was about 7 AM and the highway was deserted. With absolutely no traffic around, the car got to triple digits quickly and easily. I was cruising at about 108-ish in the right lane. Out of nowhere, this motorcycle flashed past me like I was standing still, quickly leaving me in the dust to the point where I could no longer see him. If I was doing 108, I wonder how fast he must have been going!

My use of it as a daily driver ended because I made a serious blunder purchasing a vehicle for my wife. I will discuss this in detail next week. Suffice it to say that she needed a car so, for the second time, a Caprice was relegated to baby-hauling duty.

The car served her well for a few more years, surviving a series of parking encounters with larger vehicles (and our house) which resulted in a creased fender and dented tailgate. This car actually survived and outlasted the next six COALs, which you will be reading about in the next few weeks.

In the end, it was my perpetual lack of funds to properly take care of it which led to its rapid decline from flagship to liability.

The first problem stemmed from an aftermarket alarm system. When I bought the car, I was told that the system was inoperative. A few years into our ownership, I realized that inoperative was not the correct word: It was actually only hibernating. One day it came out of its slumber. The alarm would sound at random moments and then shut off by itself. This happened maybe once every two weeks. We didn't have a fob or any other means of shutting it off, so we just let it be. The real problem came when the second feature of the alarm system became active once again. Namely, the starter interrupt feature. Without the fob, we couldn't disarm it; therefore, we couldn't start the car. At the same time, we were more broke than ever, so we didn't even have any money to tow it somewhere to have someone look at it. While we were pondering this, my wife had to walk to get to where she had to go (which entailed having to cross a busy highway; thankfully, there was a crosswalk). I finally realized that funds to fix the problem were not coming anytime soon, so for the second time since my Saab, I performed a DIY auto repair. I went through the car, pulled any fuses that were not in the owner's manual, and removed any parts that did not look stock. I also took a great risk by cutting any wires that looked out of place. Well, I was lucky. I cheered loudly as the LT1 roared back to life; I screamed and danced around in victory as my three-year-old looked on proudly.

The LT1 B-bodies had two main weaknesses. One was the 4l60E transmission, with its debatable reputation for early (and expensive) failure. Are the transmissions inherently bad due to a design flaw, or is the failure rate due to neglect and abuse? I have heard both sides. I've also heard that the 94' 4l60Es were stronger than the ones in the 95-96 B cars. The second weakness was the Optispark. What is an Optispark? The Optispark was essentially an advanced distributor that used infrared and optical sensors to operate properly. Because it was such a high-tech piece of equipment, it was not cheap. In addition, it is difficult and tedious to gain access to it. At the time, a genuine GM Optispark cost between $600-$800 before installation. In addition, like replacing a timing belt, replacing the Optispark meant replacing the water pump because water pump failure almost always meant damage to the expensive Optispark. These two components are what have led many to give up on their LT1 dreams, and probably why they are not more prolific today.

As I said, the transmission on my car held up pretty well. The oil was pink, in good shape and serviced regularly. There came a time when the car began running roughly and eventually missing, running on seven cylinders. The driveabilty issues began to worsen until it became obvious that the Optispark was failing. I did not have the $1,600 minimum needed to replace the Optispark, the plugs and the water pump, so my mechanic suggested an alternative. At the time, various companies offered "generic" equivalents to the Optispark. Some were of better quality than others, but all were considerably cheaper than the OEM part. So, I gambled. And lost. We tried replacing the part twice, both efforts ending in failure and stranding me on the side of the road.

It was heartbreaking to make the decision to cut my one-time dream car loose. This vehicle was our last GM product to date. Incidentally, after it left our service it was replaced by a vehicle that we kept until November of 2014. You'll read about that one next month..

Since I parted company with my Saab, I had been enjoying an unprecedented eight years or so of automotive reliability. This would change very quickly. My next few COALs will feature some of the worst automobile decisions I have ever made, leading to some of the darkest days in my car-owning history.

1994 Dodge Caravan – "Seeing Red and Hearing Ringing in Our Ears"

(The pictures used in this post are taken from Google images)

We had moved to a new home in the New Jersey countryside. My wife was good enough to sacrifice her career to stay home with our son and the family which we were planning to grow. The area we moved to is ideal for raising a family, and many others in the community had the same idea. As a result, playgrounds, libraries, and parks and such are full of stay-at-home parents during the week. In the meantime, our son Samuel was growing quickly, and so was our need for a vehicle to haul things around with us as he learned to walk and get around. This led me to begin to think about my wife's daily driver and its continued suitability for this task. You will recall that at this time, she was using my **91 Caprice** sedan for transporting Sam around, a task for which it had been more than adequate up to this point. However, it was beginning to feel tired and its trunk, huge as it is, could barely hold **Sam's Cozy Coupe ride on car**. At the park, all the other parents had minivans, CUVs, SUVs etc., while my wife pulled in with a **sedan that looked like a police cruiser!** While the car was pretty cool, it was becoming obvious that Sam and his parents were beginning to outgrow it.

I had recently acquired my dream car (**last week's COAL**), and I wanted her to have something nice as well.

Accordingly, I found a very clean, very nice looking 1994 Dodge Grand Caravan at a small used car lot. I drove there with my wife, and it looked just as nice as it did in the pictures online. I had my wife drive it and she really liked how it drove. The only problem was that the A/C was inoperative. They were selling the van for $2,500. I counter-offered $1,800. They said $2,300. I told them $2,000 but they had to fix the A/C. They said fine, but the $2,000 would not include a warranty.

A week later they called and said that the A/C was repaired. We went over there and sure enough, ice cold A/C. We took it for one more spin, imagining the many road trips we would take it on. Everything seemed copacetic, so we gave them the money and drove off with our first minivan.

The distance from the used car lot to our home was about 30 miles. I drove the <u>Caprice wagon</u> and my wife followed in the minivan. Three quarters of the way home, I stopped for gas. When I got out of the car, I heard it: a tapping sound in the distance. I looked up and saw that the tapping sound was coming from our new minivan. I immediately realized I had turned down the warranty in exchange for a drop in the price...in essence, I had agreed to purchase the vehicle as-is! We immediately took it to my mechanic to face the music. After changing the plugs, as well as several bottles of Lucas Oil Treatment, the tapping was silenced and the van ran smoothly. This began our very short honeymoon period with our minivan.

After owning this thing for a few weeks, I began to understand why they were so popular. It was very easy to strap our toddler into his car seat with minimal bending and back strain. We also found that we could easily get to him if we needed to without exiting the vehicle. The one thing that really impressed me was its ability to hold eight passengers, and still have plenty of room for cargo. My wagon had room for six passengers and cargo, or eight passengers and almost no cargo. This feature really impressed me, which is what led me to purchase my next vehicle.

One thing I found very interesting is that the controls and driver ergonomics were very similar to my **Plymouth Acclaim and Chrysler New Yorker.** I found out that besides being based on the venerable **K car,** the van also shared its powertrain with the **New Yorker.**

Its first long trip was to a wedding in Maryland. My wife volunteered to do the driving. I enjoyed having the third row to myself–lots of room to spread out plus the ability to get to the front seat if I had to. The van had dual A/C so I had my own personal vent blowing cold air in my face on a summer afternoon….I was sold. I was even considering buying a minivan for myself.

Unfortunately, the trip home from Maryland was not so pleasant. Everything was fine until the Check Gauges light came on. This alerted us to an overheating situation. We pulled over, I checked under the hood, there was coolant loss, but it was not obvious where it was coming from. All the hoses I could see looked intact. The radiator seemed fine, and it did not look like it was a water pump issue. So, I bought two gallons of coolant, and we limped home…having to fill the recovery tank once. Apparently there was a tiny hose underneath that I missed that was responsible for the problem.

Shortly after that incident, we were driving home from somewhere and we heard a ringing noise that sounded like a cross between an old telephone and an old fashioned cash register. It was a peculiar sound; not an electronic chime, but a mechanical metallic ringing. This was followed by loud revving noises from the engine. We realized that the van was not shifting out of low gear. The infamous **ultradrive** transmission had gone into limp mode. Shutting down and restarting the vehicle solved the problem. After that, the problem would reappear at random. The only warning we would get would be the ringing sound that always preceded the vehicle going into limp mode. Taking it to the mechanic was futile. There were no trouble codes stored in the computer, and of course, the problem could not be replicated. Again, restarting the van fixed it for a while, but this was not always practical or safe to do, especially if it happened on a crowded highway. It was really disappointing, because the van was on the cusp of being perfect for us in terms of its usefulness and practicality, and it was pretty fun to drive when it worked. In addition, we really liked the elevated driving position.

My wife used it as a daily driver for about four months. We began to avoid using it on long trips because we were afraid that it would go into limp mode at an inopportune moment. One day, my wife and son got into the car and it made a horrible grinding sound from the front end. The sound was not coming from the brakes or the engine, but it sounded like something was horribly broken. The sound was deafening once the car got to around 10 mph. In addition, the steering was sluggish and there seemed to be what felt like interference when I tried to steer. A trip to the mechanic confirmed that the front suspension and steering were facing imminent failure and as usual, the repair would cost more than what the vehicle was worth. All this a week after I had already sold the previous vehicle, **the reliable Caprice sedan.** A few weeks ago, Brendan Saur did **a write up on a 94 Caravan that was nearly identical to ours**. I was very happy (and a little jealous) when I skimmed through the comments to see that our experience was not typical and for the most part, folks found them practical and reliable.

Because I had gotten her into this and she needed a reliable car, I reluctantly gave my wife **my treasured Caprice wagon** and looked for something else for myself.

My experience with the van added two more requirements to my car search:

1) The ability to carry a third row of passengers and cargo
2) Elevated seating position/high ground clearance

I found just the thing. Unfortunately, things were about to go from bad to worse…..much, much worse. Stay tuned…

1990 GMC Suburan – "Out of the Frying Pan, Into the Fires of Automotive Hell"

A few months back (November 30, 2014 to be exact), I promised that I would share my biggest automotive mistake. That day has finally come. It is difficult for me to talk about this darkest chapter in my long history of gambling by buying questionable vehicles. I'm still feeling the financial repercussions of buying this vehicle even today, nine years later. My current vehicles are a reflection of the lessons and trauma caused by this vehicle. As you will recall, I was once thought that my Saab was the worst auto decision I ever made. That fiasco pales in comparison to the tale of woe that you are about to read.

From my previous B-Body wagons, I learned to love the feeling of body-on-frame, V8 powered rear-wheel drive. My last COAL gave me an appreciation for forward-facing third row seats that allowed for the hauling of both cargo and people. I also enjoyed the elevated driving position and extra ground clearance. As a result, I added these attributes as desirable in my next vehicle.

When I had to reluctantly give up my Caprice wagon and search for a new vehicle, I used my good experience with the B-Body as a template for my search. After searching on the internet for a while, I encountered a 1992 Buick Roadmaster station wagon for $900….perfect! I called the dealer who reported that the car had been sold but he had a few more wagons like that in stock. He then ran through what he had:

1988 Chevy Celebrity Eurosport Wagon, with 40,000 original miles. I immediately said no because it had front-wheel drive. I so regret this decision. This is the car I should have bought. I actually saw it on the lot…it was beautiful!

1988 Mercury Colony Park. I turned him down because I'd never had a Ford before and was not about to start now. It turned out to be a good decision; I saw the car and it was pretty rusty.

1988 Olds Custom Cruiser. I said no because it had the leisurely Olds 307. **Been there. Done that.**

Finally he said...1990 GMC Suburban with 145,000 miles. Now that intrigued me. It had my additional requirements of three rows for people and cargo, as well as the higher ground clearance and elevated driving position. I figured this was a truck, therefore, even more rugged and reliable than my Caprice.... an upgraded B- Body of sorts since it had essentially the same drivetrain. I thought this would be an upgrade! It even had a stand-up hood ornament. Moreover, Suburbans have a reputation to "take a licking and keep on ticking." Indeed, my parents' neighbor had an '87 Suburban, which he rarely maintained and always abused, that was still going strong at 335,000 miles with no sign of slowing down. I figured there was no way I could go wrong with a Suburban. I was so wrong about that.

The next day, we went bright and early to the used car lot. We got there early before it opened, and there it was, parked in the front row. It was two-tone black over silver with the dual "barn doors" out back. I did a walkaround and there were a few dings and the paint was faded (in the GM early 90's way) on the roof but, all in all, it looked pretty solid. I looked underneath and there appeared to be surface rust on the frame rails, but again not too bad.

The owner of the lot showed up a few minutes later and before we knew it, we were going for a test drive. The truck ran and drove very well, was fairly well equipped with AC and power windows and locks. There were three rows of bench seats, allowing for a maximum of nine passengers. However, during the test drive, the brake warning light illuminated. A little unnerved, I informed the salesman, who was riding in the back seat. He calmly said "How are the brakes?" I applied the brakes and the truck stopped safely and securely. The salesman said that it may be loose wiring...he made me jiggle the emergency brake a little and sure enough, no more brake warning light. With that little hiccup taken care of, I LOVED the driving position, the power of the torquey 5.7 liter TBI V8 and the cargo and passenger room. It only had rear-wheel drive but it came equipped with a limited slip differential and I figured it would be easier on gas than the heavier four-wheel drive version.

I was sold. I wanted to take it home that day. A deal was struck for $1,800, and we left happily and we took it home without incident. The only thing we noticed was that the doors were hard to close...but if we slammed them hard a couple of times they would stay closed, so we figured we'd get used to it.

The first harbinger of things to come came the next day when I could not remove the ignition key from the steering column. It was stuck there and was not moving. I finally called a locksmith and while waiting for him to arrive, I tried one more time to remove it and sure enough, it came out. Embarrassed, I had to call off the locksmith while he was en route. He was nice enough not to charge me. But this was only the beginning of the nightmare.

Gas prices were incredibly high during this time, pushing $4.00 a gallon. This amounted to about $50.00 for half a tank. Being that my job was 65 miles away, I knew that driving the Suburban to work everyday would not be a good idea so I took the train to work daily, driving the truck five miles to the train station for the first week after I bought it.

At the end of that week, it was time to get my new vehicle inspected so I took it to my local mechanic telling him we were going grocery shopping and would pick it up in a few hours after he was finished with the NJ state inspection.. We left looking forward to putting our newly inspected vehicle into full family service. Ten minutes after we left, my cell phone rang. It was the mechanic:

"Hello, Fred...this is Mike....you'd better get back here to take a look at this truck."

This lump formed in my throat and stomach. Here is what the mechanic found:

Two tires had glass in them
Radiator was leaking
Engine failed emissions
Engine had a misfire

All of this was minor when he told me the following:

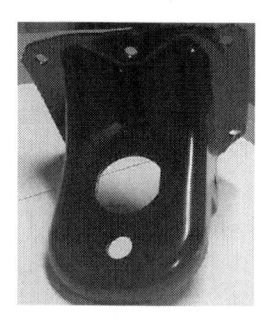

THERE WAS NOTHING HOLDING THE BODY AND THE FRAME TOGETHER….ALL THE BODY MOUNTS WERE GONE!!!

All that kept the body connected to the frame was the weight of the body and steering column. All the areas where the body mounts were installed were completely rusted away! Any jolt, like hitting a large pothole at speed, would have been enough to dislodge the body from the frame. In fact, this had already begun to occur just by putting it on the lift. And to think I had driven my wife and child in this thing!

I asked my mechanic what needed to be done to fix this. He told me that this was something he couldn't fix and his best advice to me was to get rid of the truck immediately. For some reason, I refused to accept that as an option and began looking for other places that would be willing to work with me. I quickly found that nobody in my area was willing to take this on. I should've cut my losses right then, but I was stubborn.

At work, I told a colleague my sad story. He said he knew someone who could help me, Mr. C. Mr C. owned an auto repair shop that did anything and everything. I took the Suburban to him and he agreed to fix the problems, including the body mounts.

A week later, I was looking at brand new body mounts with new metal welded in, two new tires, brand new radiator, engine tuned up, and a NJ inspection sticker. Total cost: $5,500, or three times what I paid for it! But hey , I thought, at least now I have a reliable, working truck.

I think it was home for about a week when a horrible banging noise started in the rear end. Turns out, the rear-end gears were shot! $1,300 later, again I was sure that at least I had a reliable working truck. By this time, the brake warning light was also constantly on. The brakes seemed fine, so I just put some black electrical tape over the light so its red glare would bother me no longer. Also, when first starting out, the temperature gauge would rise rapidly and almost get into the red zone and then fall back to normal. I thought this was strange but since it never overheated, I just ignored it and hoped for the best.

Early one morning as I was leaving the driveway for work. I stepped on the brake and nothing happened. The pedal went to the floor...total brake failure. Since I was just leaving, my speed was low enough that I just threw it in park to stop the truck. I stepped on the brakes again, and all was fine. So, I shrugged it off and drove to work. I would not have done this today although it actually got me to work fine without incident and I really enjoyed driving it. The drive home from work was great...until five miles from home, when the oil pressure light came on! With fear and trembling, I took it to the mechanic. Because he was really busy, he did not get to it for a few days. This led me to imagine all kinds of horrible scenarios. Finally they called me and said that they had figured out the problem: It was low on oil! They filled up the crankcase and I was good to go.

All was fine for a few weeks since I used the truck to take me no further than the train station five miles from my house. I even took my parents out to lunch in it, finally making use of the third row seat. A few weeks later, after again taking the truck to work, déjà vu set in when once more when the oil pressure light came on. This time, more extensive tests were done and it was determined that at the very least, an engine rebuild was needed! This would've cost an additional $2,500.

Utterly disgusted and nearly broke, I was completely demoralized and just didn't want to deal with it anymore, I was sick of it and just wanted out. I sold it for scrap for $200. This misadventure reminded me of a <u>COAL by Michael Freeman about his experience with an 82 Suburban</u>. Except unlike me, Michael had the wisdom to know when it was time to get out. Plus, he paid a lot less for his and got the same $200 in scrap value that I did.

Including the price of the truck, I spent close to $9,000 (not too far from the down payment I made when I bought my house) and had nothing to show for it except the $200 scrap value. I had only myself to blame... how could I have been so stupid and prideful and obsessed? Ultimately, this was THE worst automotive and arguably financial decision I have ever made!

Extremely depressed, I turned to what I thought would be a familiar, reliable solution. It turned out to be a respite from my experience with the Suburban....but a very short respite. Sometimes, that light at the end of the tunnel–is a freight train headed straight for you. Tune in next week...

1995 Buick Roadmaster and 1993 Chevrolet Caprice – "When Castles Fall"

To put it mildly, my last COAL was a traumatic, indescribable, absolute disaster...emotionally and financially. I needed something that worked and I needed it now. Because of this bad experience, I was not going to experiment with unknown products anymore. For me, B-bodies represented security, certainty, and reliability. My automotive universe was fine until I strayed from them. I would not make that mistake again–from now on, I would seek out only B-body station wagons.

The first such candidate was a 1989 Pontiac Safari with about 70,000 miles, which I thought was kind of neat because a late-model Pontiac B-body wagon is rare and unique. I also found the third-row seat interesting because it was cloth-covered. My previous wagon third seats had always had vinyl upholstery. The exterior was in pretty good shape but the interior, not so much.

The seller had a big dog who was allowed free rein inside the car. The result was that every cloth surface, including the headliner, was ripped. The more pressing problem was that the alternator warning light was on; the owner said it only needed a belt. I may have been motivated to investigate further, but the interior was so unappealing that I quickly lost interest.

The second candidate was an 85,000 mile 1995 Buick Roadmaster being sold by an auto salvage yard. The car did not have a salvage title. The only defect was a cracked windshield. It was actually in very good shape, and had a perfect blue-leather interior. I wanted this car. The problem was that the seller was very rude. He called me mentally insane suggesting that I should be institutionalized when I tried to negotiate his $7,000 asking price. He refused to budge, so that door was closed.

At this time, I was a member of an online forum that specialized in these cars. There was a member in upstate NY who bought, sold, and provided technical support for these things. He was about four hours away and there was an impending snow storm coming, but having no local prospects, I gave him a call. He was extremely pleasant and said that he had a few vehicles that would meet my budget.

His place was four hours north of me, in upstate New York, so I rented a vehicle that would take me there in comfort; the fairly newly released (at that time) Dodge Charger with the 5.7 liter V8. To this day, I remember how much I enjoyed my time with the Charger. I still wonder what would have happened if I had just bought it outright from the rental company.

Anyway, the drive up there was wonderful...the Charger was great. The only thing I did not take into account was that I was driving into a snowstorm in a rear-wheel drive, V8-powered sedan. There were a few harrowing instances when I drove through small towns with unplowed roads. Although the car did get twitchy, it never lost traction and I got there on schedule. I think the fact that I was in upstate NY among drivers who knew how to drive in the snow worked to my advantage.

When I pulled into the dealer's lot, I thought I was in B-body heaven. There were Roadmaster, Caprice, and Custom Cruisers as far as the eye could see. It was like being transported back to a 1994 dealer's lot. The owner of the dealership was warm, accommodating, and a true expert on these cars. It is a shame that this business is no longer around today.

We walked through the lot. The selection was incredible and I soon found a Dark Cherry Metallic 1995 Buick Roadmaster that I was interested in. There was one issue: It was being offered for less than half of what I was prepared to pay. I couldn't believe it! I called my wife to ask her what she thought and her response surprised me. She said "buy two of them that way we have a backup." Well, she didn't have to tell me twice...overjoyed I did exactly that. I quickly found a 1993 Caprice also in Dark Cherry metallic.

The next part of the process was choosing options. The dealer had a huge parts inventory and was willing to outfit your purchase with pretty much anything you requested, from new engines to interiors. I had factory keyless entry installed and elements of the plusher Roadmaster interior installed in the Caprice. The plan was to drive the Roadmaster home and have the Caprice shipped.

The Roadmaster was a class act. It had the same 260 hp LT1 V8 and 4L60e transmission that my 9C1 and 95 Caprice wagon had but was also equipped with automatic climate control and red leather interior as well as the towing package, which included a heavy duty suspension and limited slip differential. I would say that this is the most comfortable car I have ever had from a seating perspective. Long distance driver comfort was not an issue.

The Caprice did not have the LT1, but did have the more reliable and less complicated L05 V8 and 700R transmission. The car also had the towing package and had comfortable cloth seating. I had the dealer install a Roadmaster center armrest/console for added comfort and convenience.

Both vehicles served as my daily drivers for my long commute to work. In addition, it was the '93 Caprice that took our youngest son, Adam, home from the hospital after his birth. The cars did serve us well for a time providing comfortable, reliable transportation during that honeymoon period. Along with my wife's white 95 Caprice wagon, we now had three B-body wagons in our fleet.

I alternated taking each to work to keep the mileage and the wear down. In addition, I would take the train a few days a week. This worked for almost two years. In retrospect, that's not really a long time, but this length of service was almost five times longer than my last two COALs. In addition, the whole experience cost me less than $3,500, including the price of both cars.....way better than my last experience.

One thing that I should have realized is that while these cars were rugged and reliable, time was against them. They were aging quickly and required more looking after and were no longer fit for frontline heavy duty service because of their age and the fact that they had been out of production for over a decade, so parts and support were becoming scarcer and scarcer.

The dealer I had bought them from was ready, willing, and able to keep them running but he was four hours away. The time for their use as daily work horses was coming to a close. Slowly age conspired against them and things began to grow wrong, essentially nickel-and-diming us. My wife was wise when she told me to buy two of them because essentially, both were needed to support my grueling 120 mile daily commute.

Eventually, one of them was always out of service and in the shop. As soon it was repaired, the other one would break down. After a while, there was never an occasion when both vehicles were fit for service at the same time. Because I did not have the money to do a full overhaul on them, these cars should have been weekend projects or occasional use vehicles only and not subjected to the hard life I was asking of them. B-bodies are wonderful cars, but even they get old.

The 93 Caprice died first. First the climate control vents malfunctioned so that when the climate control was switched on, the air was blowing out of all the vents all the time with no way of controlling or regulating it. Then the radiator, alternator, and water pump had to be replaced. A few days later, the anti-lock brakes stopped working. Then about a week later, I was driving home on the highway when I experienced total brake failure. All lanes were crowded so I couldn't pull over. Traffic in front began to slow and I was going about 75. I began to pray to God for the family of the driver of the Honda in front of me who would be pulverized by my out of control full sized wagon. Thankfully, traffic began to move and I was able to pull over safely.

It turns out that a brake line had ruptured. Two days later, I was driving home and noticed a fine mist being sprayed at my rear window from somewhere beneath the car. I thought it strange but the car was running so well. Twelve miles from home, the

transmission began to slip. I
was angry because this is
the same car that stranded
me when the brakes failed
just two days before.

The wise thing to do would have
been to pull over, but I was
angry at being stranded again
by the same car, so I forced it to
take me home. It did get me
home, but never ran again.
Apparently, a transmission
line had ruptured (a
cheap fix) but my running it
without fluid destroyed the
transmission, thus ending the
car's service.

The Roadmaster did not last much longer. First, the power steering pump and lines needed to be replaced. Then the transmission oil cooler went. At first I thought that the transmission was going but it was only acting up because the fluid was leaking out of the cooler. Thankfully, the trans was not damaged. All of this happened in less than two months. The engine and trans on this car actually ran pretty strongly. The car ran better than my wife's (and my former) Caprice wagon despite the high mileage.

What did it in was that the water pump began to leak. I knew this was the end because a leaky water pump meant the Optispark's condition was questionable. The Optispark was essentially an advanced distributor that used infrared and optical sensors to operate properly. Because it was such a high tech piece of equipment, it was not cheap. In addition, it is difficult and tedious to gain access to it. At the time a genuine GM Optispark cost between $600-$800 before installation. In addition, like replacing a timing belt, replacing the Optispark also meant replacing the water pump because water pump failure almost always meant damage to that expensive Optispark.

I was looking at between $1,500-$2,000 in parts and labor. After being burned by <u>my last COAL,</u> I did not want to take it any further and repeat <u>my last mistake.</u> It turned out I made the right choice. I sold the car to someone who had plans to restore it. He e-mailed me about eight months later to let me know that he had since replaced the transmission since it failed a few months after he had taken it off my hands. He also removed the fake wood and repainted it silver. I wish I had saved that photo from seven years ago.

This left the <u>white Caprice wagon as our last surviving B-body</u> and also our last GM vehicle. It bravely soldiered on for two more years until it too succumbed to the ravages of time and hard use. Through this site, I have met folks who still have B-body wagons in service; I admire and congratulate them. These cars are disappearing quickly and I'm happy to hear that there are still a few of them out there, particularly the LT1 cars due to the idiosyncrasies of the Optispark and 4L60E transmission. My next COALs did not last as long as these cars, but served as a wake up call to rethink the way I bought cars. <u>You will read about them next week.</u>

1998 Plymouth Voyager & 1997 Ford Crown Victoria – "Wake Up Calls"

After my last experience, I had hit automotive rock bottom (again!). Here and here, my dad shared his surplus vehicles with me, and he would help me out one more time. This time, help would come in the form of a 1998 Plymouth Voyager.

Ours was the short wheelbase version. A TSB (Technical Service Bulletin) had been released about the accessory drive belt. Apparently there was a good chance of the drive belt slipping off whenever you drove through a puddle because of placement of said belt. Unfortunately, my dad had been stranded many times because of this design flaw. Fortunately for us, the <u>TSB</u> was released shortly before we took ownership of the van and Dad had the water guard and reinforced belt suggested by the <u>TSB</u> installed by the time we took over, effectively solving the problem.

Mechanically, the van was actually very reliable, the engine ran very strongly and the transmission shifted smoothly. We enjoyed the cargo room and versatility, and it became our default family vehicle along with our<u>Caprice wagon.</u>

It was a series of cascading electrical failures that proved to be this van's undoing. First, the passenger-side power window stopped operating. A few days later, before we could even address the window problem, I turned on the radio. I heard a pop and was confronted by an electrical burning smell. Needless to say, the radio was dead. I replaced the fuse but the radio did not come back–it was fried. I found out soon enough that the radio was not the only problem. All the lights on the climate control panel were blinking simultaneously. I searched online and found that it was in diagnostics mode. I learned how to reset it, but unfortunately it looked like the panel and the air conditioning were fried as well. For added fun, this occurred at the beginning of summer, leaving me a van with no air conditioning and a passenger window that would not roll down. Soon, the battery would drain whenever it was parked for a long time. The mechanic traced this to a resistor under the hood that was draining the battery. Finally, the entire instrument cluster shorted out, leaving us no warning lights and no instruments. It was time to find another vehicle.

With very little money left because of my past adventures, the plan was to buy basically a beater whose only role would be to take me to the train station so I could just take the train to work from then on. A search on cars.com revealed a very nice looking 1997 Ford Crown Victoria at a dealer less than five miles from home. Since I had experience with B Bodies, I thought I'd give the Panther platform a try. It was a hot day in late July, the sales person handed me the keys and I took it for a test drive. The 4.6 liter V8 ran smoothly, but the suspension felt a bit tired and there were some squeaks and rattles. I remember coming back from the test drive and the sales person asking me "How was the AC? Did it freeze you out?" I had to tell her the truth. The air conditioning did cool the car, but it did not "freeze me out." She said, "let me see what else we have. " Truth be told, I was willing to go with the Crown Vic but I thought it was nice of her to look.

She came up with a 1990 Volvo 700 series wagon. She did not walk me out to see the car. Instead, she just gave me the keys and told me the Volvo was right outside. I know nothing about Volvos. I can't tell one Volvo wagon from another. My last experience with a European car was my ill-fated <u>Saab</u> but I was willing to give it a try and was so glad I did. The car was loaded with everything, including a sun roof and really nice leather seats. As a bonus, in the cargo area I found two brand new tires already mounted on factory rims. The car had about 130,000 miles on it, about 30,000 less than on the Crown Vic. I took it for a test drive, and what a difference from the Crown Vic. Strong acceleration and very tight suspension, it felt very much like my <u>9C1</u>. When I got back, she asked me again "How was the AC? Did it freeze you out?" This time the answer was, "the AC was cold….meat locker cold!" With a delighted smile she said, "…so I guess you'll be taking this car home today." I said absolutely and we agreed that it would be $500 plus the van in trade just like the Crown Vic. I thought it was too good to be true but there it was…I gave her the money and they began to fill out the registration papers. All of a sudden, the sales person was gone. I sat there waiting for probably 45 minutes. I couldn't really leave because I had already given her my money and signed over the van's title. She reappeared later with an anguished look on her face.

Apparently, the 1990 Volvo 700 series wagon that she thought that she had sold me for $500 was already sold. Through some inventory error, the Volvo I had test driven was actually a 1998 Volvo 960 which cost $3,000 more! As I said, I know nothing about Volvos. She told me she would help me get financing so that I could take the Volvo home, but this simply was not in my plan so I refused. So, she said she had one more car she wanted me to look at for the agreed upon $500 plus trade.

The vehicle in question was a 1997 Lincoln Mk VIII. The car was a blue color with blue leather seats. I took it for a spin and definitely felt the power of the 280 horsepower DOHC V8. However: 1) The AC didn't "freeze me out" 2) The beautiful dash had pieces missing 3) The Check Engine Light was on 4) I had seen too many Mk VIIIs with suspension sag and feared that this may be what was awaiting me and that correcting it would not be cheap. The Crown Vic was squeaky but it had no warning lights and because it was only $500, and because I was buying any of these cars "as is," I ended up going with the big Ford. After all, I just needed it to get myself to the train station. Plus, I looked in the glove box and found that the engine was replaced at 100,000 miles, so I was really buying a 60,000 mile car. I also discovered that it had previously failed NJ State Inspection due to an illuminated Check Engine light, but since it was no longer illuminated, I assumed the problem was solved. Happily, I took it home.

I drove it blissfully for about a week. Despite the squeaks and rattles of the tired suspension, it felt smooth and powerful and was actually getting good highway gas mileage for a V8 (between 25-28 mpg without traffic). The trunk was also much deeper than my previous Caprice sedan's, and it had remote keyless entry.

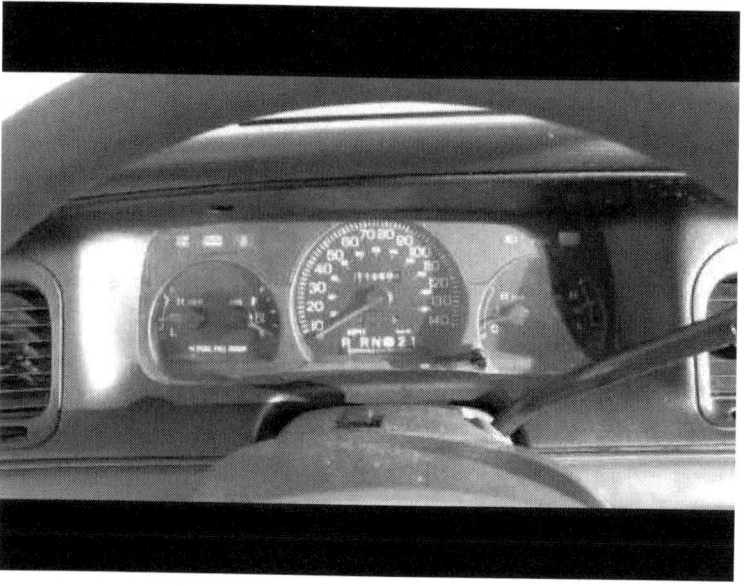

The next week, it was time to get it inspected in order to get the permanent registration and plates. In New Jersey, an illuminated Check Engine light means an automatic fail, this is why I passed on the MK VIII. No inspection=no plates. I was right about the Crown Vic: the Check Engine Light was not illuminated. There was a reason for that–the previous owner had removed the bulb! In actuality there were four trouble codes, the most expensive of which were two catalytic (cat) converter codes. This meant, of course, that the car failed inspection and that I would not be able to permanently register it until I got the items in question fixed. The estimates were between $700-$900. I discovered soon after that according to the VIN number, it was equipped with the California emissions package and would thus cost slightly more to get the cats fixed. Great–I had just gotten myself into another situation. So what did I do? I turned to Mr. C. of course. You all remember <u>Mr. C.</u> right? He was the one who helped me out with the body mounts on the <u>ill fated Suburban</u>. Here was his solution: 1) The computer was setting two catalytic (cat) converter codes 2) He could clear the codes but the inspection computer would still not be able to pass the car since the car needed to be "driven" for a period of time after the codes are reset to prevent people from cheating by just clearing the codes. 3) His solution was for me to drive the car until it passed the threshold for being "driven" and run the inspection program before the car's computer flashed the bad code again. He reasoned that the car's computer may be too "sensitive" and there may be nothing wrong with the cats….Suuuure. At this point, I was up for anything; so I would drive the car for a few hours and return to Mr. C. to see if we had achieved our objective of "sweet talking" the computer. Back and fourth I went; I must have driven over 300 miles that day. Needless, to say, this was yet another on my long list of stupid, boneheaded ideas that wasted time and yielded no results. Try as we might, the trouble codes stayed and the only way to fix it would be new cats. I did not have anything close to the amount required, so I began researching waivers to the New Jersey State Inspection. I found that I had a good case to get the waiver so I began to prepare the paperwork.

That is, until the next day when it refused to start. Turns out the fuel pump had quit… an extra $700 repair right there. Total time of ownership: five weeks. And another one bites the dust…

This vehicle is actually the straw that broke the camel's back for me. I knew it was time to rethink how and what kind of vehicles I would be buying from now on. After many years with basically the same car buying philosophy, my experiences with these cars were what finally convinced me to go in a different direction. You will see the result in my final COALs over the next two weeks.

2005 Honda Accord & 2002 Subaru Forester – "The Game Changers"

I was 36 years old. I had a wife, two kids and a mortgage, not to mention a 120-mile daily commute. I needed to take a new approach to my car purchases. What I was doing was definitely not working...it was time to balance practicality and romanticism in car buying. As much as I wanted to be the guy with the old school Curbside Classic American iron as a daily driver, I no longer had the time, money or mechanical skills to live this dream.

My good friend and mentor Dominic gently convinced me of this and slowly persuaded me that it was time to let go of some of the hard and fast rules and prejudices I had developed in terms of my preferences when buying cars, namely: 1) Only buy American 2) All four cylinder cars are weak and underpowered 3) Avoid front wheel drive 4)

Spending more than $3,000 to purchase a car is a mistake 5) With the exception of the Lexus LS 400, Acura Legend, and Acura NSX, all Japanese cars are unsafe penalty boxes. He then took me car shopping. I thought for sure this would mean a Sentra, Corolla, Civic, Neon, or Escort. I actually ended up being happy with what awaited me, a 2005 Honda Accord LX in Graphite Pearl.

The Accord was a certified pre-owned car with 44,000 miles. I was very impressed with the high quality interior. While not ostentatious, it was functional and quite comfortable. I especially liked the electroluminescent gauges which were very classy, but they did take some getting used to. Since the dashboard was always lit up, I had to remember to turn on the headlights at night! The only thing really missing was an auxiliary jack for my MP3 player.

It had the VTEC DOHC 2.4 liter four-cylinder engine with 160 hp. Handling was very good, and acceleration was not bad. However, I do remember manually downshifting a few times to improve performance which the owner's manual said was OK to do. Remember I was coming from **V8-equipped** cars. When I wasn't manually shifting, shifts with the five-speed automatic were so smooth as to be virtually undetectable. At 34 MPG, gas mileage was better than anything I'd ever owned before.

Overall, it seemed very solid and well built. One thing that was refreshing in light of my past few experiences was the fact that the car needed nothing except for oil changes and new tires. Absolutely nothing went wrong with the car. I was never in fear of it stranding me. The last time I had a car this reliable was my **old Acclaim**, except that the Honda was much more fun because it was peppier, more comfortable, and got better gas mileage. I also owned this car during the last few months of my Grandma's life so it helped to not have to worry about the car failing me when I needed to get to the hospital. Because our only other car, the **Caprice wagon**, was ailing and no longer reliable, we ended up taking the Accord everywhere, subjecting it to frequent and heavy use where it served faithfully and reliably.

The only reason we replaced it is because frankly, we used it way too much, putting almost 40,000 miles on it a year. Another year of driving would put it over 100,000 miles. After going through some harrowing times with **my last few COALs**, I was a little wary of pushing my luck, especially since this was my first Honda. I do remember checking the online forums to see how reliable Accords of this generation were after 100,000 miles. At the time, they were still fairly new so there were not too many with higher mileage, like mine. Because of my inexperience with Hondas, we traded it in for next week's COAL. In retrospect, knowing what I know now, I could have easily kept it, and it would probably still be running and trouble-free today. I still miss this very refined and balanced car.

Since my wife was still driving **my old Caprice wagon,** it had become obvious that retiring that venerable platform was inevitable. A solution soon emerged as my in laws were upgrading their vehicles, so my wife took over their 2002 Subaru Forester and our **Caprice wagon** passed into history. This marked the first time in 7 years that we did not have a **B-body** on duty. The Forester was a well equipped S model with the Cold Weather Package, which meant heated front seats, side mirrors, and limited slip differential.

Under the hood was a 2.5 liter four-cylinder with 165 hp. I found the engine quite brawny, with very strong acceleration. At 23 MPG, gas mileage was not much better than the [Caprice wagon](#) it replaced. In addition, it had a relatively small gas tank, which limited its cruising range.

The interior, while not as comfortable as my Accord's, was quite robust, able to withstand anything two small children could dish out. We also liked the heated front seats, a feature my Accord did not have. The frameless windows were also interesting.

While not as commodious as the <u>Caprice wagon</u> it was replacing, we found the cargo area spacious and versatile. There was also a power outlet in the rear cargo area. It was pretty cool, because it was the perfect place to plug in our air pump to pump up the kids' bicycle tires, footballs and basketballs.

The two things I most appreciated about the Forester were its 7.5 inches of ground clearance and AWD capability. Indeed, we used it during many a snowstorm, and it never left us stuck, even in weather that immobilized our other cars.

In terms of maintenance and repairs, it needed the most attention at 90,000 miles. Maintenance items included the timing belt, spark plugs, transmission fluid and engine coolant. A word about the last item. These engines had a reputation for eating head gaskets if the coolant was not changed regularly and a special Subaru coolant additive added at the prescribed intervals. Many sources I have read indicated that head gasket failure was inevitable due to poor design. Thankfully, this never happened to us in the 145,000 miles that we owned it. Repair items included wheel bearings and oil leaks.

The most memorable thing that happened was when Hurricane Sandy struck New Jersey in 2012. The day the storm was predicted to make landfall, I moved the car from where it was parked under an older oak tree to a space close to, but not underneath, a tall pine tree. That night, the storm arrived with a vengeance! There were sheets of torrential rain, high winds–and within ten minutes of the storm's arrival, the loss of electrical power.

Twenty minutes later, we heard the beeping of the Subaru's factory alarm system. We stared in shock and horror at the surreal sight outside of our window. We saw the eerie glow of the Subaru's flashing parking lights underneath the branches and leaves of the pine tree that had fallen on top of the Forester! I immediately apologized to my wife, since I had decided to park the car in that spot–thinking that it would be out of the way of any falling trees! I immediately told her that she could have my car (next week's COAL).

The next morning, we went outside to face the music. The photos above are exactly what we saw the first thing that morning. It did not look good. While I could not see any broken glass, it looked like the main portion of the pine tree had come cashing down on the roof of the car. We could not see the extent of the damage because it was obscured by tree branches and leaves.

New Jersey was in a state of emergency. We were without power for close to a week, gas was being rationed, trees were down everywhere, and many people were left homeless. Because of this situation, it took a few days to get anyone to remove the tree from our car. When the day finally came, we waited with bated breath as the layers of leaves, branches and the tree trunk were removed. When the last of the tree was removed, we were shocked and speechless when we saw the worst of the damage to our Subaru: a small dent in the roof and a few scratches on the roof rack. It was quite miraculous. The car was fine. We were driving it within minutes of its extraction from underneath the tree. I'm still amazed to this day!

The car served us faithfully for almost six years. I believe it stranded us only once, when the battery connections were frayed and needed replacement. When it hit the 144,000-mile mark, it needed about $2,000 worth of work. Two oxygen sensors, brake rotors and pads all around, exhaust system replacement and CV boots. Also, the second (expensive) timing belt change interval was looming just around the corner, and I was still afraid of the engine's reputation for head gasket failure at higher mileage. In November 2014, we made the decision that it was time to move on.

These two cars were game changers. They were our first Japanese cars. They also ushered in an era of amazing vehicle reliability—a trend continued by our current vehicles, which you will read about next week.

2010 Honda Accord & 2013 Honda Accord – "The Biscayne & the Bel Air"

If you have been following my series, you know that of the many COALs I have written about, the most numerous and best were the full sized GM sedans and wagons; the B bodies. I have been driving for 26 years and have owned B-bodies on and off for close to half that time. In their heyday, they were ubiquitous because of their reliability, competence, versatility, economy, comfort and performance. Everyone including families, cab drivers, captains of industry and police offices relied on them. They were always ready to complete yeoman's tasks with minimal fuss and maximum reliability.

Chevy used a particular nomenclature to differentiate the level of equipment and luxury of its flagship sedans. The Biscayne was the lowest-priced and least-equipped model; the Bel Air was the midrange model; and the Impala, and later Caprice, represented the top of the line.

I submit that the Honda Accord now fills a role similar to the legendary large GM B body sedans of the past. This post is so titled because I see the Accord as a sort of demonstration of of why so many people bought B-bodies. Indeed, I liken the Accord buyers of today to the Chevy buyers of yore; families looking for reliable, cost effective transportation; on the other hand, Acuras remind me of Buicks or Oldsmobiles: more luxurious and refined than the Chevy, but with the same underlying goodness and offeering dependable, reliable motoring.

The Big Honda.

There is big, and there is big. So you may not think the Honda Accord is a big car. After all, it's only 162.8 inches long. And that's a good deal shorter than the Chevrolet Monza's 178.6 inches.

But the outside dimensions of a car don't always tell you how big it is inside. And that's where the Accord may surprise you.

Like all Hondas, the Accord has a transverse-mounted engine with front-wheel drive. This means the engine is tucked away up front, out of the way, and there is no drive shaft to the rear wheels. The space we save by this configuration is turned over to our passengers in the form of roominess and comfort.

With the rear seat folded down, the Accord converts to a roomy cargo carrier. And its hatchback design permits easy access to the fully-carpeted rear deck.

Regardless of its size, the Accord is definitely big on standard features.

Its base sticker price includes AM/FM radio, automatic maintenance reminder and electronic warning system, tachometer, steel-belted radial tires, rear window wiper, washer, and defroster, and our CVCC engine, which runs on regular or unleaded gasoline.

Right here we would like to reassure you on one point. Although we fondly refer to the Accord as the Big Honda, it is only big by our standards. We don't build what are traditionally called big cars. And we don't intend to start.

A big car wouldn't be as simple to park as the Accord. Or as simple to maneuver in city traffic. And if we can't make it simple, we don't make it.

HONDA
We make it simple.

I find it interesting that the Accord started off as a compact car for the yuppies of the era and has evolved into a daily workhorse for families and commuters. How would people have reacted in 1976 if they were told that someday, the Accord would replace the Bel Air, LTD and Newport as the go-to family sedan?

My first Accord, the 7th generation 2005 model mentioned in **last week's COAL**, was an experiment–apparently a very successful one, since I put 40,000 trouble-free miles on it the first year I owned it.

Hence, it was replaced with an eighth-generation 2010 Honda Accord LX in Polished Metal Metallic: my first brand new car. Often derided, the eighth-generation Accords (2008-2012) were the largest Accords to date and were classified as full-size cars. I remember when I first test drove it that I immediately took a liking to its large interior...it was good to be back in a big car. The LX trim level was the base level and for 2010, in terms of mission, cost, and equipment, it was definitely akin to an old fashioned Biscayne. The interior, while roomy, was definitely decontented. Gone were the classy flourishes I'd gotten used to in my last Accord, which was also a base-level LX. Gone were lighted power window switches, extra ambient lighting, console tray, lighted glove box and engine trimming.

Despite its austere level of equipment, I was impressed with it as a whole. As I said, the interior was very roomy and its drivetrain smooth and responsive. It came with the base engine, a VTEC DOHC 2.4 liter inline 4 with 177 HP, which was more HP than in my <u>last Accord</u>. It also came equipped with a very smooth five speed automatic. There is a bit of disagreement on this, but I found it faster and smoother than <u>its predecessor</u>. It also came standard with traction control and Vehicle Stability Assist (VSA)

I took delivery of it the week before Christmas 2009. Because of the holidays, I put 744 miles on it in my first week of ownership. We traveled down to Maryland for Christmas, and this is where it really impressed me. I loved the stereo. This was the first time I had a factory stereo with an auxiliary jack for my MP3 player. Plus, the stereo played MP3 discs and had steering-wheel stereo controls. The leg room and elbow room were perfect for a long drive, especially with the kids aboard. I felt like I was back in my <u>Caprice</u>.

No wood trim on my car

Our two small kids, their luggage, plus their Christmas presents (which included a small bicycle) ALL fit in this larger Accord. Initially, we were worried that all the stuff would not fit and we would have to leave a few items behind, but everything fit nicely.

I was surprised how much snow came down in the Baltimore-Washington DC metro area. It looked like upstate NY. Anyway, the Accord with its Vehicle Stability Assist and Traction Control did better than my brother-in-law's CRV, which ended up stuck in his driveway, as well as his neighbor's Suburban which was stuck in the middle of the street! I was very apprehensive, but the Accord managed to get through their unplowed street with no issues whatsoever! It may be an illusion, but it also seemed that my new Accord had more ground clearance than <u>my previous one</u> since the bumpers seemed to line up more with my brother in law's CRV, which may have helped in the snow. On stock tires, my <u>2005 Accord</u> was mediocre in the snow. I felt much more confident in the 2010 and its stock Dunlops although getting out of a parking spot after an overnight snow was still an issue when we got over 4-5 inches of snow.

I was actually quite happy with this car as my daily driver and our family road trip car. Gas mileage was very good. One summer, we drove from Central New Jersey to Bar Harbor, Maine (550 miles) without refueling. Only two things about the car really annoyed me. The first was that road noise at highway speed was very noticeable. I have read that this is a common Honda complaint. The second issue I had was that the stock headlights were dim and inadequate at night, particularly in winter when I had a few close calls due to visibility. I rectified this by installing HID headlights, which were a huge improvement over the stock units. There was one problem. Somehow, this caused the **TPMS** light to come on as soon as the HIDs were on for a half hour or longer. I'm told that an upgraded headlight wiring harness would solve this but I didn't bother.

I had a few mishaps with the car, all occurring during the winter. The first one happened when I'd had the car for less than a month. A large icicle fell from our roof overhang, impacting and denting the top of the right fender. A few years later, in a freak late October snowstorm, the rear fender was clipped by an inexperienced snow plow driver. Thankfully, we were able to repair the body damage issues at little to no cost.

I never had any mechanical problems with the car in almost four years of ownership. Major maintenance items came down to rear brake pads and transmission fluid.

When the car was approaching 100,000 miles, I was contacted by my local Honda dealer about upgrading to the new ninth-generation Accord. How could I say no?

Accord LX

www.HondasAcuras.com   Basque Red Pearl II

If the 2010 Accord LX was a Biscayne, its replacement, a 2013 Accord LX, was a Bel Air. When the 2008-2012 eighth-generation Accord was released, the word was that Honda was slipping. The car's larger dimensions were criticized as ungainly and bulbous. In my opinion, the criticism to the car's look was similar to the criticism given to the [1991 Caprice](). In addition, the low-tech decontented interiors were also criticized, especially in light of the well-equipped cars from Hyundai and Kia. Honda responded with the current ninth-generation Accord.

For roughly what I paid for my 2010 Accord, my 2013 model in Basque Red Pearl II was indeed an upgrade. Even though it was a base model LX, it came with a backup camera, Bluetooth, Pandora radio integration, extra ambient lighting, USB port, traction control, CVT transmission with sport and economy modes, alloy wheels, external temperature display, fuel economy computer and dual-zone automatic climate control. All standard. Along with the CVT, the DOHC base four cylinder now had 185 HP and 181 lb./ft. of torque. Honda had indeed stepped up their game. The level of technology on this car is light years ahead of anything I have ever owned...and it all works reliably! Just to be sure, the dealer threw in a 120,000 mile extended warranty and free oil changes for the next three years. I find the backup camera most useful. Accords have short and thus hard-to-see rear decklids, so backing in was always a pain since I couldn't see where the trunk ended. The backup camera has completely solved this problem.

I have to say I love this car. I drive 120 miles a day; the car is not only comfortable, but when driven gingerly on the highway with no traffic, manages 36-40 MPG. Shift the CVT into sport mode and it pulls almost as strongly as my 9C1 did. The car is slightly smaller than the previous generation but I don't mind since it is better equipped, faster, more fuel efficient and more nimble. Plus, the trunk is actually larger than the old car. I have owned it a little less than two years and have put about 60,000 trouble-free miles on it. This winter has been brutal in New Jersey. Sub zero temperatures and wind chills, piles of snow, and icy roads have been the norm around here lately. I have come to regard my Accord as excellent in the snow. I'm not sure if it's the weight ratio, the stock Continental tires, or the traction control, but I've not gotten stuck once this winter. I've had issues with my last two Accords when getting out of a parking spot after an overnight snow storm. This has not been an issue at all with my current Accord. In fact, we just got eight inches of snow and there was no need to dig out to provide traction or ground clearance go to work in the morning, I just put the car in gear, backed up, and left. I dare say that thus far, I do not miss the All Wheel drive traction of my Subaru.

Accord LX

www.HondasAcuras.com   Basque Red Pearl II

I ended up trading in my last two Accords at about 100,000 miles even though there was really no reason to do so. I think this Accord will be different because I will not be trading it in early. It is just about perfect for me. It is comfortable, sporty, economical, very well equipped and fun to drive. This is easily the best car I have ever owned. As Jim Klein put it at the end of his COAL series…. "My daily driver is a keeper."

Post Script: 2014 Honda Civic

My wife's <u>2002 Subaru Forester</u> featured last week served us for over five years and at 145,000 miles needed about $2,000 worth of work, not to mention a known design flaw that allows the head gasket to become susceptible to failure at higher mileage. It was Thanksgiving weekend 2014, and we decided to check out the holiday offers and ended up with a 2014 Honda Civic LX. Like the Accord, it came very well- equipped for a base model, sporting both a backup camera and Bluetooth. Since I compared my last two Accords to a Biscayne and a Bel Air, what would the Civic be? A Nova or a Chevelle?

In the short time we have owned it, my wife appreciates the much improved fuel economy over the Subaru as well as the technology such as the backup camera and Bluetooth. She does miss the storage capacity that the Subaru offered. On my part, I think the two-tiered dashboard takes some getting used to, but I do appreciate the build quality and very competent road manners. It is still very new to us so we are still getting to know it.

This concludes my COAL series. I have enjoyed sharing the

times of my life as they relate to the cars I have loved or not loved. I am filled with a sense of gratitude as I reflect back on my life. I have been surrounded by wonderful people, great experiences and great cars. Thank you for giving me the opportunity to do this, and I hope you have enjoyed hearing about my Cars of a Lifetime!

In case you missed them, here they are again in order of ownership, by owner:

Ed's Cars:

1968 Buick Opel Kadett
1974 Chevrolet Vega
1970 Pontiac Firebird Esprit
1978 Datsun B210
1983 Toyota Tercel
1982 Mercury LN7
1982 Datsun 210
1986 Hyundai Excel
1993 Toyota Camry
1995 Ford Crown Victoria Police Interceptor
1992 Toyota Corolla
1998 Nissan Altima
1998 Toyota Corolla
1999 Toyota Corolla
1969 Mustang Grande
1957 Chevrolet Bel Air

Fred's Cars:

1984 Buick Century & 1981 Buick Skylark

Poorest Quality: 1985 Chevrolet Cavalier, 1984 Chevrolet Cavalier, 1984 Pontiac Sunbird

1976 Chevrolet Camaro

Most Memorable: 1978 Chevrolet Caprice Classic

Rarest (Have not seen one of the same year in 20 years): 1986 Pontiac Grand Am

Most Embarrassing: 1985 Chrysler LeBaron & 1987 Chrysler New Yorker Turbo

Least Reliable/Most Unusual: 1983 Saab 900

Most Surprising: 1988 Dodge Aries

1992 Plymouth Acclaim (Most reliable cheap used car) & 1991 Chrysler New Yorker

1998 Chevrolet Cavalier

1991 Chevrolet Caprice

Most Fun: 1995 Chevrolet Caprice 9C1

1992 Buick Roadmaster

1988 Chevrolet Caprice Classic

Most Beloved: 1995 Chevrolet Caprice Classic

Weirdest Experience: 1994 Dodge Caravan

Most Life Threatening/Scariest: 1990 GMC Suburban

1995 Buick Roadmaster & 1993 Chevrolet Caprice Classic

Shortest Ownership: 1998 Plymouth Voyager and 1997 Ford Crown Victoria

2005 Honda Accord LX & 2002 Subaru Forester S- **Toughest**

2010 Honda Accord LX, 2013 Honda Accord LX (**The Best I've Ever Owned**), & 2014 Honda Civic

Conclusion

In conclusion, an interesting note about our combined expenses on our fine collection of cars? About ½ million U.S. dollars. And remember, many of those dollars were spent "back in the day." So who knows what the true inflationary cost would be in today's dollars. Although, it was worth the memories!

We owned 45 cars and last that we checked, we're still alive!

Made in the USA
Charleston, SC
29 June 2015